12

D0932309

Martin Kramer
EDITOR-IN-CHIEF

Using Benchmarking to Inform Practice in Higher Education

DISCARD

Barbara E. Bender
Rutgers University

John H. Schuh
Iowa State University

EDITORS

Number 118, Summer 2002

JOSSEY-BASS
San Francisco

USING BENCHMARKING TO INFORM PRACTICE IN HIGHER EDUCATION
Barbara E. Bender, John H. Schuh (eds.)
New Directions for Higher Education, no. 118
Martin Kramer, Editor-in-Chief

Microfilm copies of issues and articles are available in 16mm and 35mm, as well as microfiche in 105mm, through University Microfilms Inc., 300 North Zeeb Road, Ann Arbor, Michigan 48106-1346.

New Directions for Higher Education is indexed in Current Index to Journals in Education (ERIC); Higher Education Abstracts.

ISSN 0271-0560   electronic ISSN 1536-0741   ISBN 0-7879-6331-3

NEW DIRECTIONS FOR HIGHER EDUCATION is part of The Jossey-Bass Higher and Adult Education Series and is published quarterly by Wiley Subscription Services, Inc., a Wiley company, at Jossey-Bass, 989 Market Street, San Francisco, California 94103-1741. Periodicals postage paid at San Francisco, California, and at additional mailing offices. Postmaster: Send address changes to New Directions for Higher Education, Jossey-Bass, 989 Market Street, San Francisco, California 94103-1741

SUBSCRIPTIONS cost $60 for individuals and $131 for institutions, agencies, and libraries. See ordering information page at end of book.

EDITORIAL CORRESPONDENCE should be sent to the Editor-in-Chief, Martin Kramer, 2807 Shasta Road, Berkeley, California 94708-2011.

Cover photograph and random dot by Richard Blair/Color & Light © 1990.

Jossey-Bass Web address: www.josseybass.com

Printed in the United States of America on acid-free recycled paper containing at least 20 percent postconsumer waste.

CONTENTS

EDITORS' NOTES

Declining confidence in the academy, combined with increasing scrutiny of higher education by funding agencies, legislators, and the public has compelled academic leaders to improve the extent to which their colleges and universities are meeting goals. The Wingspread Group on Higher Education report (1993), for example, asserted that "Public confidence in the 'people running higher education' has declined as dramatically with respect to education leaders as it has with respect to the leadership of medicine, government, and business" (p. 6).

Taylor and Massy (1996) suggest that given the extraordinary challenges facing higher education, governing boards and senior leaders of educational institutions need to develop new ways to demonstrate the accountability of higher education. They stress that institutions of higher education need strategically developed indicators that "provide an honest assessment of how an institution is doing and where it is heading" (p. xi). They also suggest that appropriate and realistic benchmarks will "enable decision makers to assess an institution's strategic position through comparative analysis" (p. xii).

Benchmarking, a tool that has been used for years in industry, is one approach that higher education leaders can employ to measure the extent to which institutional goals and objectives are being met. To do so effectively, institutions will need to ensure that they are comparing themselves with the proper benchmark institutions. Rush (1994, pp. 84–85) indicates that benchmarking attempts to answer the following questions:

- How well are we doing compared with others?
- How good do we want to be?
- Who's doing the best?
- How do they do it?
- How can we adapt what they do to our institutions?
- How can we be better than the best?

Academic leaders who employ benchmarking techniques must make sure that they compare themselves with select institutions that have similar characteristics. Discussing the importance of benchmarking with appropriate institutions, Upcraft and Schuh (1996, p. 241) stressed that "The key here is to choose institutions, functions, and processes which are comparable to your own." Such dimensions as institutional control (public or private), mission, Carnegie classification, and region of the country are examples of factors that could influence the selection of peer institutions.

The institutional mission can affect "all aspects of the day-to-day institutional life and the future growth and development of the college or university" (Barr, 2000, p. 25), so accurately identifying that mission is imperative in benchmarking. For example, it would make no sense to compare the admissions practices of a public institution that uses an open admissions policy with a selective independent college that relies heavily on SATs.

This volume provides multiple perspectives on the use of benchmarking in higher education. The authors present a conceptual overview and organizational examples of how benchmarking can be used in colleges and universities. Our expectation is that the reader will develop an appreciation of benchmarking as an administrative tool, including a greater awareness of its strengths and limitations. We also hope that administrators or faculty members in higher education will be able to develop their own strategies for using benchmarking.

In Chapter One, Marya Doerfel and Brent Ruben present a comprehensive view of benchmarking. They include best-practice approaches to organizational assessment and improvement in higher education, and they conclude with lessons that can be gleaned from the benchmarking process.

John Schuh describes the use of the Integrated Postsecondary Educational Data System (IPEDS) in Chapter Two. As Schuh demonstrates, the IPEDS relational database can be useful for making informed comparisons of institutions of higher education.

Chapter Three, by Loren Loomis Hubbell, Robert Massa, and Lucie Lapovsky, discusses the use of benchmarking in managing enrollment. Using a case study, they illustrate how benchmarking can help administrators develop strategies for planning and implementing admissions and pricing practices.

In Chapter Four, Robert Secor describes how joining the Big Ten influenced the use of benchmarking at Penn State; it meant more for Penn State than intercollegiate athletic competition.

Richard Novak explores the use of benchmarking in distance learning in Chapter Five. Given the growing popularity of distance learning, Novak stresses that creating meaningful benchmarks is particularly important not only for institutions, but also for regional accreditation associations.

In Chapter Six, Robert Barak and Charles Kniker describe how governing boards can use benchmarking to provide direction for colleges and universities. They include a number of examples from several states.

Robert Mosier and Gary Schwarzmueller discuss the use of benchmarking in student affairs and focus on issues related to student housing in Chapter Seven. They provide contemporary institutional examples of how benchmarking has influenced administrative practice at many institutions.

In the final chapter, Barbara Bender considers the role of campus leaders in the benchmarking process. She notes that without the commitment of college and university leaders, any attempt to address accountability issues through benchmarking will be futile.

The authors provide a wide range of ideas and concepts pertaining to benchmarking. As higher education leaders respond to more demands of the academy, effective benchmarking can make a difference in the decisions pertaining not only to budget allocations, but also to the existence of academic programs. We hope that this volume will help institutional leaders consider the ways that benchmarking can be used to influence the planning, implementation, and evaluation of activities to enhance the quality of programs and services in contemporary higher education.

Barbara E. Bender
John H. Schuh
Editors

References

Barr, M. J. "The Importance of Institutional Mission." In M. J. Barr and M. K. Desler (eds.), *The Handbook of Student Affairs Administration*. (2nd ed.) San Francisco: Jossey-Bass, 2000.

Rush, S. C. "Benchmarking—How Good Is Good?" In W. F. Massy and J. W. Meyerson (eds.), *Measuring Institutional Performance in Higher Education*. Princeton, N.J.: Peterson's, 1994.

Taylor, B. E., and Massy, W. F. *Strategic Indicators for Higher Education*. Princeton, N.J.: Peterson's, 1996.

Upcraft, M. L., and Schuh, J. H. *Assessment in Student Affairs: A Guide for Practitioners*. San Francisco: Jossey-Bass, 1996.

Wingspread Group on Higher Education. *An American Imperative: Higher Expectations for Higher Education*. Racine, Wis.: Johnson Foundation, 1993.

BARBARA E. BENDER is associate dean of the graduate school at Rutgers University.

JOHN H. SCHUH is professor and chair of educational leadership and policy studies at Iowa State University. He was a fellow at the National Center for Education Statistics in summer 2000.

1

This chapter presents an overview of benchmarking as well as dashboard indicators for higher education.

Developing More Adaptive, Innovative, and Interactive Organizations

Marya L. Doerfel, Brent D. Ruben

The information age and the global economy have brought new challenges and opportunities to organizations in all sectors. The changes have forced organizational theorists and practitioners to question what constitutes ideal organizing and organization. Innovative and expansive thinking is required today, more so than at any previous time. Managers, employees, vendors, and consumers bring new expectations to the work environment—expectations that span sectors and geographic boundaries. Technological advances that permit at-home banking, for example, have created new expectations and opportunities for at-home shopping, at-home travel planning, and at-home auction bidding. Similarly, increased attention to customer friendliness in the entertainment, retailing, or hotel industry creates new expectations in health care and education. The scientific organization that Taylor (1911) idealized simply does not apply in the organizational milieu of the twenty-first century, as organizational managers—as well as employees—find themselves forced to regularly rethink their roles, expectations, behaviors, and even the nature of their industry. Contemporary organizational leaders no longer can rely on traditional business practices: they must now engage in cross-organizational and cross-sector learning in order to survive and prosper. Opportunities—even necessities—for dramatic change have permeated all sectors. Even institutions of higher education—"ivory towers" so named for their tradition of independence—have begun to engage in new levels of organizational self-examination and have adopted effective practices from other institutions and other sectors.

Benchmarking in higher education is the foreground of this chapter, but we also examine theoretical issues concerning models of best business

NEW DIRECTIONS FOR HIGHER EDUCATION, no. 118, Summer 2002 © Wiley Periodicals, Inc.

practices. In the first part of this chapter, we take a communication perspective that provides a systems theory approach to defining the process of benchmarking. We give an overview of recent developments in assessing and managing organizational knowledge vis-à-vis semantic network analysis. Next we discuss recent benchmarking practices while we draw on interorganizational communication theory to provide clarification on how and why organizations cooperate despite their competitive nature. We then focus on the institutions of higher education, and on initiatives within many colleges and universities that use benchmarking to foment and guide organizational change. Subsequently, we discuss the growing impact of benchmarking concepts and approaches in higher education, and focus on two particularly noteworthy approaches to organizational assessment and improvement in higher education—the Malcolm Baldrige (National Institute of Standards and Technology, 2000b) and "balanced scorecard" (Kaplan and Norton, 1996) frameworks—approaches that have grown out of, and are now dramatically contributing to, benchmarking theory and practice. The chapter concludes with strengths, weaknesses, challenges, and lessons learned as well as more generic shortcomings and critical issues associated with benchmarking.

What Is Benchmarking?

Jackson and Lund (2000) note that benchmarking definitions vary depending on the perspective. In the introduction to their volume on benchmarking in the United Kingdom, they argue that benchmarking involves comparing organizational or industry practices, performance, and process in order to improve the focal organization or business. Other scholars, such as Schuler (1998), define benchmarking as "a structured approach for looking outside an organization to study and adapt the best outside practices to complement internal operations with new, creative ideas" (p. 40).

Specific subcategories of benchmarking also have emerged. Yarrow and Prabhu (1999) differentiate three forms of benchmarking: metric, process, and diagnostic. Metric benchmarking seems to be the simplest and most straightforward in that it compares the performance data of businesses. Though efficient and simple, the metric process requires that the businesses are comparable, and it focuses only on superficial manifestations of business practices. Process benchmarking refers to an expensive, time-consuming endeavor in which two or more organizations complete an in-depth comparison of specific business practices in order to achieve better results (see also Camp, 1995; Zairi, 1992). Diagnostic benchmarking, on the other hand, "is more akin to a 'health check' for the company, helping to identify which practices need to be changed and the nature and extent of performance improvements which should be followed" (Yarrow and Prabhu, 1999, p. 794).

Upcraft and Schuh (1996) list three types of benchmarking practices in higher education: internal, competitive, and generic. Internal benchmarking refers to making comparisons between units within the institution. Competitive and generic benchmarking refer to identifying best practices of other organizations. Competitive benchmarking involves comparisons with direct competitors, whereas generic benchmarking involves organizations that are not direct competitors but share similar organizational practices and procedures.

Publications oriented to both academic and practitioner readers emphasize that benchmarking is a *process*. Taking the process approach to benchmarking, Shoham and Fiegenbaum (1999) argue that the procedures an organization espouses to employ performance-enhancing strategies are more important than the strategies themselves. Fundamentally, the benchmarking process is one of comparison. It identifies and learns from analogical comparisons between the activities, strategies, methods, or outcomes of one's own organization and those of other organizations.

Comparisons may focus on organizational inputs, internal processes, or outputs. The exact nature of these categories varies, of course, depending on the level of analysis and kind of organization under consideration. In the context of higher education, for example, comparisons can be made at the level of an institution, department, program, workgroup, or specific process. And one may compare across academic, support, or administrative units. At an institutional level of analysis, one might examine recruiting relationships with junior colleges (inputs), organizational approaches to planning (internal processes), and student placement and faculty publication (outputs). Or, at a lower level of analysis, a university computing services department could benchmark vendor management (inputs), the management of on-campus computer labs (internal processes), or approaches to assessing student or faculty satisfaction with services (outputs). Or, an academic department could benchmark approaches to recruiting top graduate students (inputs), methods for assisting faculty with research and publication or providing professional development for staff (internal processes), or student satisfaction (outputs). As noted earlier, these comparisons can be with other higher education organizations, or with other sectors. For instance, the computing services could benchmark against other higher education institutions, or with computing organizations in private sector, governmental, or health care organizations.

Common to all these circumstances are two primary reasons for which benchmarking is undertaken. Perhaps the most typical goal of benchmarking is *assessment*. Comparing one's own organizational activities with those of others provides a context to make better sense of one's own outcomes and achievements. Suppose, for example, that a survey of students' satisfaction with computing services on a particular campus revealed that 65 percent of first-year students were "extremely favorable" or "somewhat favorable" in their rating of computing services. What, exactly, is the significance of this finding? It offers little value for assessing one's own performance without having a context in which to interpret the finding. Benchmarking provides that context. Comparisons with peers, competitors, or leaders provide the basis for interpreting one's own results in a meaningful manner. If comparable, competitor, or leading computer services departments at similar institutions achieve a rating of 50 percent on these criteria, then we arrive at quite a different conclusion than if the average rating was 80 percent.

Innovation is a second value of benchmarking. Comparing one's own organization to others can provide new insights into ways of thinking and working, and inspire and motivate useful and profound change. Organizational leaders often report that some of their most creative organizational insights come from benchmarking what might seem the least likely comparisons. Thus, for example, members of a product-oriented organization might find they are stimulated by new ways of thinking about customer service through comparisons with a service-oriented business. Or, officials might find inspiration in faculty recruitment by benchmarking with private-sector research and development organizations.

Contemporary Uses of Benchmarking

In marketing, accounting, management, and business communication journals, one can find academic reports on benchmarking that discuss

- Lessons learned from fast-growing industries such as Internet companies (Fine, 2000)
- How organizations determine who to benchmark (Cox, Mann, and Samson, 1997; Elnathan and Kim, 1995)
- Cooperative benchmarking and determining the organizations to include in the partnership (Elnathan and Kim, 1995)
- Survey reports that provide comparisons of various best-practice approaches (Terziovski, Sohal, and Moss, 1999)
- Critiques of the fad nature of myriad best-practice models (Abrahamson and Fairchild, 1999)

Although some accuse benchmarking of being yet another craze in the acronym-littered world of business assessment (Abrahamson and Fairchild, 1999; Rigby, 2001), benchmarking practices began in traditional organizational environments—environments in which businesses find survival, growth, and market dominance consistently more difficult as the global market and new business forms (such as Internet companies) have become a presumed presence. For example, Xerox is regularly referred to as the significant benchmarking trailblazer. In the 1970s, the organization looked to its competitors for models of business practices (Camp, 1989). Since then, authors such as Cox, Mann, and Samson (1997) suggest that two themes have emerged in the benchmarking literature: "the value of learning from contexts outside an organization's usual frame of reference, and the growing importance of undertaking this learning using a structured, formal approach" (p. 286). Moreover, when one realizes that benchmarking is, at its core, simply another name for comparison, it is apparent that although there may be something faddish about the term, there's nothing faddish about the practice.

The paradigm of comparison and information sharing in organizational development has found its way into other organizational settings such as health care (Dewan, Daniels, Zieman, and Kramer, 2000), human resource management (Bamberger and Fiegenbaum, 1996; Sanchez, Kraus, White, and Williams, 1999), and in academia—the focus of this volume. Benchmarking studies consider financial issues (Fine, 2000; Dopuch and Gupta, 1997; Morling and Tanner, 2000; Troutt, Gribbin, Shanker, and Zhang, 2000) and focus on organizational relationship processes often associated with human resources management, training and development, and organizational knowledge—including how these areas affect organizational performance (Browne, 2000; Fitz-enz, 1993; Glanz and Daily, 1992; Longnecker, Stansfield, and Dwyer, 1997; Pfeffer, 1994; Sanchez, Kraus, White, and Williams, 1999).

Early benchmarking studies have been criticized as vague and ambiguous and an invalid means for identifying organizations that demonstrated best practices (Fitz-enz, 1993). Although in Fitz-enz's initial assessments, organizations emerged as having demonstrated—with verifiable data—that they constituted excellent organizations, Fitz-enz also found that such organizations' results were often contradictory (1993). They were disregarded with a seemingly obvious and theoretically sound explanation: best practices are context-sensitive (American Productivity and Quality Center, 1999; Jarrar and Zairi, 2000). For example, Jarrar and Zairi argued that "'best' is a moving target in today's world, and is also situation-specific" (p. 735). Fitz-enz pointed out that whereas two organizations emerged as exemplars, their specific data on a given topic were diametrically opposed. "For example, compensation positioning might be totally different; that is, above versus below the industry mean; and yet both companies showed exceptional control of compensation expense" (p. 21).

Unlike authors of studies who report case-by-case results based on various output data, Fitz-enz delved back into his data and realized that a common thread ran through these traditional markers of best practices. The organizations he studied shared a common set of "qualities and values that support—and indeed drive—their decisions of what to do" (p. 21). He theorized that whereas practices such as total quality management are visible activities, the key characteristic that enabled the organization to emerge as a best-practice example is the organizing philosophy that drives its practice. That is, Fitz-enz noted that best practice "is not a set of discrete actions but rather a cohesive, holistic approach to organizational management that is the antecedent to and transcends the visible activity" (p. 22). At the core of Fitz-enz's foundations are concepts that reflect the systems theory philosophies of interdependence, holism, and environmental influences. Among eight qualities he outlined, the first five either imply or specifically idealize systems components: (1) communication with employees (interdependence), (2) continuous improvement (feedback), (3) organizational culture (holism), (4) customer focus and partnering (environmental influences), and (5) interdependence and cooperation.

In effect, Fitz-enz underscored the value of philosophies related to systems thinking as tantamount to success; he stresses that it is the commitment to the philosophy—not a specific practice such as benchmarking or total quality management—that drives organizational successes. "It's not 'Quality' this month and 'Benchmarking' next month and 'Reengineering' the month after that. If they go into 'Quality,' they go all the way. If they get into benchmarking, they make the commitment to learn how to do it right" (p. 25). He concludes that his data strongly suggest "that performance is human—not system or model or even resource—driven. High performance and best practices are the result of vision, aspirations and skills of individuals who choose to be excellent performers" (p. 26).

Whereas Fitz-enz's contribution provides a generalized theory of organizational excellence, books, academic articles, and practice-oriented publications are evidence that benchmarking is here to stay. Unlike Fitz-enz's harsh critique—that business reports historically have been irresponsible in generalizing claims that are merely case-specific—there are benchmarking studies that delve more deeply than the earlier metric-focused analyses. For example, in their attempt to understand how to transfer knowledge learned from benchmarking practices—and when such transfer is appropriate— Jarrar and Zairi address more theoretical conditions that preclude any successful transfer. They argue that to adopt best practices appropriately, organizations need to embrace permanency in their strategies, commit to its adoption, recognize necessary additions to the infrastructure, and include teams that will endure beyond the benchmarking life span. Jarrar and Zairi focus on the underlying factors of a successful benchmarking experience rather than the manifestations that are being simulated. The processes that drive successful organization change often are the focus of communication and network research that until now have not been discussed in tandem with benchmarking.

Thus, benchmarking can refer to comparisons at various levels. It can be used to refer to rather superficial comparisons such as how many times phones should be allowed to ring before they are answered in a service center (which are highly situation-specific), to processes through which organizational assessment is conducted (which are much more generic and transferable). This helps explain differences in perspectives regarding the value of benchmarking and also points to an important theoretical and pragmatic concern for organizations that wish to undertake the practice.

Making the Micro-Macro Link. In his benchmarking study on human resource management, Browne (2000) notes that there are no benchmarking studies that link employee-level issues to organization-level outcomes. In his appeal for benchmarking of human resource management (HRM) practices to include employee-level outcomes, he suggests that "it is questionable if truly progressive HRM practices can be identified if the benchmarking effort fails to address the other side of the production equation (employee-level outcomes). HRM practices are progressive only if the concern for organizational-level outcomes is matched by a concern for the well-being of employees who are directly affected by these practices" (p. 55). Though Browne's point is valuable, it is only nominally accurate. An unfortunate oversight has happened because academic studies on relational issues in organizations do not explicitly identify their diagnostic and predictive models as *best business practices* or *benchmarking*. Cross-fertilization from field to field, though sadly absent, answers Browne's critique that studies are lacking the micro-macro link.

The same arguments—that relational issues impact organizational outcomes especially in a dynamic and competitive global market—are explicit and implied in research that connects relational issues such as social capital and networks with organizational outcomes such as individuals' influence (Manev and Stevenson, 2001), managing information and retention after layoffs (Susskind, Miller, and Johnson, 1998), turnover (Feeley and Barnett, 1997; Krackhardt and Porter, 1986), and holding a competitive edge (Branscomb and others, 1999; Monge and Fulk, 1999). These studies identify the locus of information in an organization and identify where gaps lie. The findings of these studies echo the same concerns as benchmarking research when they identify issues at the relational level (such as social influence, uncertainty reduction, or a move to decentralized decision making) that have profound impact on organization level survival, growth, and innovation (Ulijn and others, 2000). They are organizational assessments that emphasize and document (benchmark) the driving processes that facilitate thriving organizational practice.

Focusing on internal assessment, Martin (2000) argues that corporate knowledge is a resource to be banked and used toward growth and innovation. And benchmarking inside an organization contributes to organizational knowledge. Benchmarking the organizations' knowledge gives a reflective sense of corporate potential and identifies vacuums. Though Martin considers the mapping of knowledge within the organization at Hughes Space and Communications, such mapping can be seen as part of a more recent development in an area referred to as semantic networks (Doerfel, 1998). Semantic networks research has used network analysis tools to map knowledge based on organizational members' communication about the organization. Moreover, semantic network analysis provides information on who knows what, and where the missing links of information and knowledge are located within the system.

Scholars have argued that use of documents such as the text of employee interviews or published writings by members of an organization provides robust and in-depth information that traditional surveys fail to provide (Danowski, 1982; Doerfel, 1998; Doerfel and Barnett, 1999; Freeman and Barnett, 1994; Lievrouw, Rogers, Lowe, and Nadel, 1987; Monge and Eisenberg, 1987; Rice and Danowski, 1993). Such information can be mapped out, and strengths and weaknesses of organizational knowledge can be identified. For example, Lievrouw and others (1987) used this technique to identify "invisible colleges"—individuals who function as members of a knowledge network within an organization—who were pursuing similar yet distinct lines of research in biomedical science that would otherwise have not been recognized. Doerfel and Barnett (1999) assessed dominant themes of scholarship in the communication field by analyzing topics of presentations at the annual meetings of the International Communication Association. Rice and Danowski (1993) used semantic networks to identify distinct types of information technology users.

The use of semantic networks in such academic studies is similar to Martin's (2000) call to 'bank' organizational knowledge, in that the depiction (as an organizational output) and distribution of knowledge among the organizational members influence innovative practices. Martin posited that knowledge is a business output that can facilitate an organization's innovativeness or be a detriment to its progress, and that knowledge as a focus in today's organizations can be attributed in part to "globalisation and the interaction of technological and organizational change. . . . knowledge is not just an input to business today but frequently it is the output and objective of the company" (p. 18). Semantic network analysis offers a valuable form of internal benchmarking that contributes to organizational growth by identifying established areas of expertise, areas where growth is needed, and missing domains of expertise.

The Competitive-Collaborative Paradox. At the core of external benchmarking lies an incongruity: organizations often look to their competitors for models of best practice. Dating back to early twentieth-century organizational philosophers such as Taylor (1911) and Weber (1947), organizational research has historically reflected inward—not outward—in assessing the organization. Furthermore, the nature of competition makes the idea of sharing information complex. Benchmarking scholars have considered the equivocality when identifying the *who* and *how* of benchmarking engagement (Cox and others, 1997; Elnathan and Kim, 1995; Jarrar and Zairi, 2000). Information sharing and cooperative competitors have research and theoretical explanations that predate the practice of benchmarking (Axelrod, 1984; Burt, 1992; Pfeffer and Salancik, 1978).

The philosophy of benchmarking can be attributed to organizational theories, including institutionalization, game theory, and resource dependence theory. Taken together, these theories offer a framework for understanding the circumstances in which businesses find themselves involved in an emerging cooperative relationship with organizations they might previously have considered their competition. This does not imply that organizations are breaking collusion laws, but rather, research has seen the emergence of new organizational forms such as networked organizations (Miles and Snow, 1986, 1992) and cooperative behaviors among competitors (Brandenburger and Nalebuff, 1996), especially in the face of new challenges and heightened uncertainty as the economy favors global and turbulent markets. Thus, a theoretical understanding of the emergence of cooperation proves useful for organizations who want to engage in external benchmarking endeavors.

Institutionalization theory purports that organizations that do business "right" become the ideal. In some cases, they emerge in the vernacular because their dominance results in such product recognition that their name is a better identifier of the product than the generic term. Until recently, we "Xeroxed" our copies, and still use the terms Kleenex (facial tissue), Band-Aids (bandages), and Scotch tape (cellophane tape)—all products whose labels are the institutionalized brands, now synonymous with the products they represent. Similarly, organizations whose reputations are tantamount to the business ideal because of their internal dynamics become idealized models. Institutionalization theory proposes that these high-profile reputations advance the legitimacy of the organizations (DiMaggio and Powell, 1983; Euske and Roberts, 1987). The theory of institutionalization posits that such external profiles mean that organizations must adhere to the pressure to conform, specifically, "that organizations conform to the expectations of the environment by adapting 'appropriate' (rational) structures and behavior. . . . In response, the organization is deemed legitimate by its environment and receives needed resources (financial, support, generalized acceptance)" (Euske and Roberts, 1987, p. 58).

Institutionalization helps explain the organizational ideal and the social pressures of organizational conformity. However, the traditional view of competition—that it is a zero-sum game—reminds us that looking to other organizations for best practices implies that the other has the competitive edge. According to resource dependence theory (Burt, 1992; Euske and Roberts, 1987; Galaskiewicz, 1979; Pfeffer and Salancik, 1978) organizations exist, thrive, and survive in environments in which opportunities and constraints can be highly influential. Specifically, resource dependence theorists argue that an organization's interdependence with others can be "altered in two ways: (1) they can absorb the other entities or (2) they can coordinate with other organizations to achieve mutual interdependence" (Euske and Roberts, 1987, p. 52).

Thus, there is an undeniable tension between competition and cooperation that must be addressed in benchmarking. There are instances when organizations might ideally like to benchmark with their competitors who may be cautious in sharing information (DeVito and Morrison, 2000; Cox, Mann, and Samson, 1997; Yarrow and Prabhu, 1999). At the same time, the quest for best-practice rewards like Malcolm Baldrige, a new business practice model, has matured from a zero-sum business strategy to a paradigm that embraces win-win outcomes (Brandenburger and Nalebuff, 1996).

According to game theorists (Axelrod, 1984), for cooperation—even among competitors—to begin, a single player (organization) needs to take one small step. What can emerge, then, are the collaborative benefits in which all involved are able to enjoy win-win outcomes. Whereas inter-organizational network scholars theorize on how cooperatives evolve and study the dynamics of competitors working together (see also various chapters in Nohria and Eccles, 1992), specific benchmarking studies present analyses and descriptions of how organizations determine to whom they should turn as partners and how to transfer organizational knowledge once they engage in benchmarking (DeVito and Morrison, 2000; Elnathan and Kim, 1995; Yarrow and Prabhu, 1999). Like the inter-organizational theories discussed above, these authors agree that the emergence of cooperative relationships in benchmarking ventures are indeed a challenge and require delicate management because of the paradoxical competitive environment.

Consistent with the suite of theories discussed above (resource dependence, game, and institutionalization), the common theme in the specific analyses of benchmarking partners is that engaged firms experience a survival incentive (resource need), which is often marked by a need to reduce uncertainty, which results in a search for partners with whom to share information. However, Cox and others (1997) propose that the likelihood of collaboration is related to whether the initiator is some third party versus an actual benchmarker. They suggested that a mediating organization enhances the information sharing experience that is at the heart of successful benchmarking endeavors.

These fundamental elements of benchmarking (knowledge assessment, cooperative-competitive alliances, and a systems- and process-oriented approach to organizing) have a long tradition of use and acceptance in higher education. One might argue that the concept of benchmarking was born in education. Whether one thinks in terms of the assessment of students' performance on exams, the productivity and impact of faculty research, or the quality of an academic department's systematic comparisons with peers, recognizing competitors and leaders is fundamental. The remaining sections of this chapter hone in on the practice and applications of benchmarking in higher education, illustrating the theoretical framework discussed above.

Benchmarking in Higher Education

Whereas comparison is a time-honored tradition, the term *benchmarking* and the application of the concepts to organizational assessment and innovation is a more recent development. The past few years have seen the growth of centers on many campuses devoted to identifying, adopting, and adapting effective organizational practices from other institutions and sectors. The National Consortium for Continuous Improvement in Higher Education (NCCI)—formed in 1999—brings together higher education academics and administrators from approximately sixty member institutions to "advance administrative and academic excellence in higher education by identifying, promoting, supporting, and sharing effective organizational practices among member institutions" (Ruben and Sandmeyer, 2001, p. 36). Benchmarking also has been the focus of numerous presentations, panels, and conferences in many professional organizations; volumes such as Upcraft and Schuh's (1996) multifaceted collection of student affairs assessments; and more recently, Jackson and Lund's (2000) collection, which canvases benchmarking of administrative units, library and information services, and student learning experiences.

Assessment and Improvement in Higher Education

Of the many noteworthy examples that illustrate benchmarking's value for higher education, we will focus on two: the Malcolm Baldrige and the Balanced Scorecard frameworks, both first developed for use in the business sector. They are two particularly interesting examples of innovations in higher education assessment and improvement that have come about through—and at the same time promote—systematic approaches to benchmarking. Both examples reflect the theoretical background discussed in the first half of this chapter. The principles that drive Malcolm Baldrige and the Balanced Scorecard underscore the theoretical concepts of organizational knowledge, the emergence of cooperation, and a systems-based paradigm that drives the organizational practice.

Malcolm Baldrige Framework. The Malcolm Baldrige National Quality Award Program (MBNQA) was established in 1987 by Congress through passage of Public Law 100–107. Named after former Secretary of Commerce Malcolm Baldrige, the program was created to promote U.S. business for the advancement of the national economy (National Institute of Standards and Technology, 2000a). In the years since its inception, the program has had a dramatic influence on efforts to identify and encourage the application of core principles of management and organizational quality.

The Baldrige framework sets forth guidelines for organizational excellence, against which an organization can be assessed or compared. In general terms, the model has seven categories that reference and call for cross-organizational comparison, spanning topics such as leadership strategy, organizational mission, performance measurement, workplace climate analysis, and client satisfaction. Since its introduction, the Baldrige program has been an extremely powerful and pervasive force in organizational improvement efforts. In the thirteen years since the creation of the Baldrige program, more than seven hundred organizations have submitted applications for awards, and nearly fifty have received recognition for their accomplishments (Broadhead, 2000). Among the companies that have been selected as recipients of the national Baldrige awards in recent years are large and well-known corporations such as the Ritz-Carlton Hotel Company

(1999), Boeing Airlift and Tanker Programs (1998), and Xerox Business Services, and smaller companies such as Sunny Fresh Foods (1999) and Texas Nameplate Company, Inc. (1998). In addition, the Baldrige framework serves as the prototype for award programs in forty-three states (National Institute of Standards and Technology, 2002). Many leading companies and a number of governmental organizations have also adapted the award criteria to their own needs. Above all else, the pervasive influence of the Baldrige has occurred because it provides a clear and coherent way of conceptualizing and assessing organizational excellence.

The benefits realized by the business, health care, and education versions of the Baldrige were developed and tested in 1995; forty-six applicants were in health care and nineteen applicants in education. Basically, the pilot involved translating and adapting core concepts and principles of organizational excellence to the contexts of health care and education. The education Baldrige was designed for use by educational units at all levels and all types—public and private. It was intended to be expansive enough to include kindergarten through twelfth grade systems, community and junior colleges, four-year colleges and universities, even corporate educational programs or centers. In 1998 the two new Baldrige programs received the necessary approvals and funding, and they have now been fully implemented on a national level, with many states also adopting these new awards.

Within higher education, Belmont University, Northwest Missouri State University, and the University of Missouri–Rolla have played an early and visible leadership role in applying the Baldrige framework to institutional assessment. More recently many other institutions have participated in the program in various ways. In 2001, the University of Wisconsin–Stout was the first higher education institution to receive a national Baldrige award. The Baldrige approach is also having an increasingly significant impact on professional school and regional accreditation models. The influence has been apparent in business, engineering, and the health sciences for several years; more recently the framework has also begun to have a significant influence on the approaches used by the regional accrediting associations. The North Central Association has recently introduced a new optional accreditation process called the Academic Quality Improvement Project, which mirrors the Baldrige approach in a number of respects (Biemiller, 2000). On other fronts, the National Association of College and University Business Officers (NACUBO) also developed an awards framework emphasizing the leadership and process dimensions of the Baldrige. In 1999, the American Council on Education (ACE) introduced an awards program drawing on concepts reflecting the Baldrige framework.

A further extension of the Baldrige program is the Excellence in Higher Education (EHE) program that was developed specifically for colleges and universities. (Ruben, 2001). The EHE framework uses language familiar to the culture of higher education, and is designed to be easily adaptable to the mission of any institution—or of any academic or administrative unit within an institution (Lehr and Ruben, 1999). Because the education Baldrige was intended to be inclusive and appropriate for school systems of all kinds and at all levels, the primary focus of the framework is on instructional activities and outcomes. However, unlike elementary and high school systems, many higher education institutions have missions that also emphasize scholarship and research, public service, and other functions. The EHE model was designed to provide the flexibility necessary to accommodate the mission balance of the full range of colleges and universities, as well as the full range of academic and administrative departments within these institutions.

Like the Baldrige model on which it is based, EHE consists of seven categories (Ruben, 2001). Each of the first six categories—Leadership, Planning, External Focus, Information and Analysis, Faculty and Staff Focus, and Process Effectiveness—corresponds to what is viewed as a critical component of, and a contributor to, the excellence of an educational organization. Outcomes, trends, and comparisons with peer and leading institutions are the focus of the seventh category, Excellence Levels and Trends. Collectively, the categories and the many interactions between them define a systems framework that can be used to conceptualize and analyze the workings, effectiveness, strengths, and improvement needs of a higher education department, program, or institution.

The EHE program has been implemented with approximately fifty academic and administrative departments at a number of colleges and universities, including the University of Wisconsin–Madison, University of California–Berkeley, University of Illinois, University of Massachusetts, University of San Diego, University at Buffalo (SUNY), California State University–Fullerton, the University of Pennsylvania, Marygrove College, Howard University, Miami University, MIT, and Rutgers University. Participating academic units have included law, nursing, business, engineering, education, liberal arts, communication, public policy, information and library studies, environmental and agricultural science, provost's executive councils, and graduate schools, among others. Student life and support organizations that have participated include residential colleges, housing and residence life, student campus centers, and student learning centers. A number of senior level administrative and business leadership groups have also participated, as have departments of computing services, facilities and maintenance, research and sponsored programs, human resources, police and public safety, and others.

Participants report that the Baldrige and EHE frameworks are useful tools for facilitating communication, benchmarking within and across units and institutions, providing cross-sector learning, highlighting organizational strengths, identifying and prioritizing areas for improvement, broadening faculty and staff engagement in higher education planning processes, providing baseline measures and a standard of comparison using an accepted assessment framework, and increasing the institutional commitment to change and advancement (Ruben, 2001).

Balanced Scorecard Framework. One of the defining themes of contemporary organizational theory and practice is the emphasis on information for assessing, tracking, and promoting excellence. Typically, business and industry have measured organizational performance using a financial accounting model that emphasizes profitability, return on investment, sales growth, cash flow, or economic value added. But in recent years, there have been questions regarding the preoccupation with this restricted set of measures. Constraints of conventional financial performance indicators in business (1) are too historical; (2) lack predictive power; (3) reward the wrong behavior; (4) are focused on inputs and not outputs; (5) do not capture key business changes until it is too late; (6) reflect functions, not cross-functional process within a company; and (7) are given inadequate consideration to difficult-to-quantify resources such as intellectual capital (Brancato, 1995).

The general conclusion is consistent with theories and concepts discussed earlier in this chapter. Specifically, financial indicators alone are limited in their ability to adequately represent the range of factors associated with organizational excellence. Accounting-based measures, for instance, may not capture key elements of an organization's mission, customer satisfaction and loyalty, employee satisfaction and turnover, employee capability, organizational adaptability or innovation, environmental competitiveness, research and development productivity, market growth and success, and other important company-specific factors (Brancato, 1995; Kaplan and Norton, 1996). Put another way, we must go below the surface of such indicators and emphasize the systems approach to organizational process.

Many major corporations now link financial indicators with other measures that reflect key elements of their mission, vision, and strategic direction. Collectively these "cockpit" or "dashboard" indicators are used to monitor and navigate the organization in much the same way a pilot and flight crew use the array of indicators in the cockpit to monitor and navigate an airplane. The usefulness of these indicators extends beyond performance measurement and contributes to self-assessment, strategic planning, and consensus on goals and directions within the organization.

One approach that addresses this need in a systematic way is the "balanced scorecard" developed by a study group composed of representatives from major corporations including American Standard, Bell South, Cray Research, DuPont, General Electric, and Hewlett-Packard (Kaplan and Norton, 1992, 1993, 1996). As described by Kaplan and Norton (1996, p. 2), "The Balanced Scorecard translates an organization's mission and strategy into a comprehensive set of performance measures that provides a framework for a strategic measurement and management system." Beyond simple measure performance (metric benchmarking), Kaplan and Norton emphasize organizational coordination and strategic planning as well as performance monitoring. Creating these measures is a process.

In higher education, as in business, there are time-honored traditions in the measurement of excellence. Rather than emphasizing primarily financial measures, higher education historically has emphasized academic measures. Motivated, as with business, by issues of external accountability and comparability, measurement in higher education has generally emphasized those academically related variables that are most easily quantifiable. Familiar examples are student and faculty demographics, enrollment, grade point average, scores on standardized tests, class rank, acceptance rates, retention rate, faculty-student ratios, graduation rates, faculty teaching load, counts of faculty publications and grants, and statistics on physical and library resources.

As important as the traditional indicators are, these measures fail to present a comprehensive image of the current status of an institution. They do not reflect some of the key success factors for a college or university, nor do they capture many of the dimensions of a university's mission, vision, or strategic directions.

Traditional indicators are subject to other limitations as well. Many of our most popular and familiar measures capture inputs; unfortunately, these do not provide useful information on what our institutions contribute. Measures of student qualifications and institutional selectivity are classic examples. Student grade-point averages and standardized test scores may be good descriptions of the capabilities students bring with them to our institutions, but they say little about the value of our courses, programs, or institutions, nor do they help evaluate the cumulative benefits derived from having attended. Higher education assessment outcome studies (Astin, 1993) have contributed to our understanding of the teaching and learning process, but resulting measurement frameworks have generally not been translated into indicators that are useful for monitoring, intervening in, or comparing institutional excellence (Johnson and Seymour, 1996).

As has been the case in business and other sectors, variables that are less obviously focused on academics, less tangible, or less readily susceptible to quantitative analysis have been bases for measurement less frequently. Thus, dimensions such as impact, value, relevance, need, accessibility, subject-matter competence, or motivation for lifelong learning are not widely used indicators of excellence, though few would disagree with their centrality to the academic mission of most colleges and universities.

Absent from this and many other lists of higher education performance indicators are measures that inspect the student, faculty, and staff expectations and satisfaction levels, despite the widely shared view that attracting—and retaining and nurturing—the best and brightest people is a primary goal and critical success factor. Whereas colleges and universities may gather information from students as to their satisfaction with particular courses and services, less attention has been devoted to systematically measuring expectations of prospective students and their parents or the extent to which those expectations are met or altered over the course of the college experience and thereafter. Far less attention is typically devoted to measuring faculty and staff satisfaction levels within particular units or the institution as a whole, though this may be one of the better predictors of the quality of instruction, research, administrative, and support services within an institution.

As with business, higher education indicators have tended to be primarily historical, limited in predictive power, often incapable of alerting institutions to changes in time to respond, and lacking adequate attention to important but difficult-to-quantify dimensions. Ironically, the emphasis on easy-to-quantify, limited measures has, in a manner of speaking, "come home to haunt" in the form of popularized college rating systems with which educators generally are frustrated and critical. But these are used consistently as the measures against which universities are evaluated by their constituents.

Building on the preceding framework, a university's mission, vision, and goals may be translated into dashboard indicators with five indicator clusters, each composed of a variety of constituent measures. Some are quite traditional, others less so:

• *Teaching and learning*. In the proposed framework, instruction is composed of quality assessments in two primary areas—programs, courses, and student outcomes.

The model points to the value of incorporating multiple dimensions, multiple perspectives, and multiple measures in evaluating the quality of programs and courses and student outcomes. Appropriate to these assessments are systematic inputs from peers and colleagues (at one's own and perhaps other institutions), students (at various points in their academic careers), alumni and alumnae (providing retrospective analyses), employers and graduate directors (providing data on workplace and graduate or professional school preparation). Each group can contribute pertinent and useful insights; collectively, these judgments yield a comprehensive and balanced cluster of measures that help address concerns associated with a reliance on any single perspective of measure (Williams and Ceci, 1997; Trout, 1997). Colleagues from one's own or another institution, for example, can provide useful assessments of instructor qualifications and the scope, comprehensiveness, rigor, and currency of course content. Students and alumni can provide valuable assessments of the clarity of course or program expectations, curricular integration, perceived applicability, instructor delivery skills, enthusiasm, interest in students, accessibility, and other dimensions.

In the case of the program or courses, the indicators of excellence—or *cascade of measures*—might well include clarity of mission of programs or courses, disciplinary standing, need, coherence, rigor, efficiency, qualifications of instructors, currency and comprehensiveness of course materials, adequacy of support services, and the teaching-learning climate.

Student outcome could include measures of program and course preferences, selectivity, involvement, learning outcomes (knowledge and competency acquisition), fulfillment of expectations, satisfaction, retention, preparedness, placement, and motivation for lifelong learning, and other variables that may be appropriate to the mission, vision, and goals of the institution or program. Preference measures, for instance, would document answers to questions such as: "Was this college or program my preferred choice?" Selectivity would reflect input measures of the quality of students enrolled in courses and programs, and learning outcomes assessment would measure cognitive and behavioral competencies. Thus, in addition to content learning, assessment might also include the ability to engage in collaborative problem solving, appreciation of diversity, leadership skills, interpersonal and presentational communication skills, ethical thinking, and other capabilities appropriate to the mission, vision, and goals of the institution or program.

- *Scholarship and research*. Research and scholarship involve assessments of quality in the areas of *productivity* and *impact*. In the areas of research and scholarship, colleges and universities generally have well-developed measures of achievement.

Typically, productivity indicators include the activity level. Depending on the field, activity level measures would encompass frequency of presentations, performances, article and paper submissions, publications, and funding proposals. Impact measures for research and scholarship typically include publication rate, selectivity and stature of journals or publishers, citations, awards and recognition, editorial board membership, peer assessments of scholarly excellence, funding of research, and others (Carnegie Foundation for the Advancement of Teaching, 1994; Braskamp and Ory, 1994).

- *Public service and outreach*. The *public service and outreach* indicator cluster would be composed of measures of the extent to which the university, unit, or program addresses the needs and expectations of key external stakeholder groups. This cluster should include measures for each of the groups whose assessments of the performance of the institution or program have important implications in terms of mission fulfillment, reputation, recruitment, economic viability, and so on.

The definition of *key* external stakeholder groups depends on the nature of the institution or unit and its mission. Generally, for academic units, the list of potential candidate groups would include the university (beyond the unit itself), profession or discipline, alumni and alumnae, potential students, organizations or individuals seeking new knowledge, family members or parents of students, employers, community, state, region, governing boards, friends of the institutions, donors, legislators, and the public at large.

Once the scope of key stakeholders is defined, the measures for each should capture the quality of contributions of the unit based on *criteria of significance to the external group* and reflecting *their* perspective. Some general measures that are appropriate for a number of these stakeholder groups are activity level, selection for leadership roles, reputation, meeting perceived needs, and satisfaction level.

• *Workplace satisfaction.* In addition to indicators associated with instruction, scholarship, and service and outreach, another important indicator is workplace satisfaction—for faculty and for staff. Inputs to indicators for each group could include measures of attractiveness of the institution as a workplace, turnover, compensation, assessments of workplace climate, and faculty and staff morale and satisfaction.

• *Finances.* The final set of indicators are financial and include revenues by source, such as state appropriations, tuition, donations, endowments, grants, and so on, and expenditures—operating budgets, debt service, credit rations and ratios, deferred maintenance and expenditures for the university or unit. Clearly, the specifics appropriate to this indicator would vary substantially depending on the level and type of unit involved.

The list of five dashboard indicators—and specific measures suggested for each—should be regarded as suggestive. Depending on the mission and goals of the college or university, the appropriate components of the dashboard might be quite different. Moreover, administrative units' dashboards indicator clusters would be quite different from those of academic units. Indicators for instruction and research, for instance, would be replaced by measures appropriate to the unit's particular mission. For instance, the "top row" indicators would include measures of activity and satisfaction for all units within (or outside) the university for whom services are being provided by the department. Thus, for example, physical plant departments would include measures of the satisfaction of those departments for which they provide maintenance, building, or renovation services. University communications department indicators would likely include activity, impact, and satisfaction measures from the perspective of administrative departments within the university, administration, faculty and staff, and local media for whom they provide services.

Having an established set of measures that operationally define "excellence" for an institution or unit is of great value for assessment and tracking over time. For the institution as a whole or particular units within, they provide the basis for a straightforward, accessible, and mobilizing answer to the question: "How are we doing?" To provide a context for interpreting indicator data, benchmarking and comparisons with peer, competitive, and leading institutions or units are essential.

The balanced scorecard approach lets an institution formulate a cascade of measures to translate the mission of knowledge creation, sharing, and usage into a comprehensive, coherent, communicable, and mobilizing framework for external stakeholders and for one another. As pressures for performance measurement and accountability mount, the balanced scorecard or dashboard approaches offer higher education a useful way to benefit from developments in other sectors. At the same time, the resulting tool is one that promotes and benefits from cross-institutional and cross-sector comparisons. Reflecting the first part of this chapter regarding the underlying theoretical forces, however, the identification of metrics alone may ultimately be less important than the process by which organizational members come to value and engage in self-reflection and external comparison.

Strengths and Weaknesses of Benchmarking

Benchmarking is no longer solely an assessment of financial and performance-based metrics. It is the recognition that the underlying processes that fuel performance have a profound and lasting impact on organizational success, survival, innovation, and growth. Over the past century, organizations have experienced a paradigm shift away from the insular world of Taylor's scientific management into dynamic and interactive practice. Universities and their units look to their peers as they are faced with "tougher competition, shrinking markets, and declining profits" (Voss, 1993, p. 38).

Benchmarking in higher education is limited by the same challenges as comparisons in other sectors, especially in selecting appropriate benchmarking partners. Specifically, universities must pay particular attention that their benchmarking partners share similar procedures, structures, missions. "Caveat emptor," Fitz-enz (1993, p. 19) warned, and as Ball and Wilkinson (1994) stressed, "Higher education institutions are not football teams, they have differing institutional missions and operate in different environments" (p. 427).

Conclusions

Despite the array of criticism and useful cautions that have been voiced, benchmarking and other strategies for assessing and improving quality have, and will continue to have, great value. In the final analysis, it is important to remind ourselves once again that the term *benchmarking* and some of the current methods and applications in organizations may be new, and therefore subject to the usual lifecycle of management fads and fixes. On the other hand, the underlying concepts and goals are anything but new or revolutionary; they have a long tradition of application in our work in higher education.

When it comes to innovative thinking, boundary-spanning inquiry, and a commitment to continuous experimentation and improvement in all that we do, we can and should expect the higher education community to take the lead. As always, the challenge is to differentiate *substance* from *superficiality* in our efforts to advance the quality of the work of our academic and administrative programs, departments, and institutions. Like corporate organizations, higher education institutions are susceptible, even vulnerable, in the emerged global economy. To survive and prosper we must engage in a paradigm shift that involves cooperative (despite competitive) relationships; looking outside our boundaries; and transforming our institutions and departments into more adaptive, innovative, and interactive systems.

References

Abrahamson, E., and Fairchild, G. "Management Fashion: Lifecycles, Triggers, and Collective Learning Processes." *Administrative Science Quarterly,* 1999, *44,* 708–740.

American Productivity and Quality Center. "What Is Benchmarking?" [www.apqc .org/best/whatis.cfm]. 1999.

Astin, A. W. *What Matters in College?* San Francisco: Jossey-Bass, 1993.

Axelrod, R. *The Evolution of Cooperation.* New York: Basic Books, 1984.

Ball, R., and Wilkinson, R. "The Use and Abuse of Performance Indicators in UK Higher Education." *Higher Education,* 1994, *27,* 417–427.

Bamberger, P., and Fiegenbaum, A. "The Role of Strategic Reference Points in Explaining the Nature and Consequences of Human Resource Strategy." *Academy of Management Review,* 1996, *21,* 926–958.

Biemiller, L. "North Central Association Unveils an Alternative Accreditation Plan." Chronicle of Higher Education, Apr. 21, 2000, p. A43. [http://chronicle.com/ daily/2000/04/20000040304n.htm].

Brancato, C. K. *New Corporate Performance Measures.* New York: The Conference Board, 1995.

Brandenburger, A. M., and Nalebuff, B. J. *Co-Opetition.* New York: Doubleday, 1996.

Branscomb, L. M., Florida, R., Hart, D., Keller, J., and Boville, D. *Investing in Innovation.* Cambridge, Mass.: MIT Press, 1999.

Braskamp, L. A., and Ory, J. C. *Assessing Faculty Work: Enhancing Individual and Institutional Performance.* San Francisco: Jossey-Bass, 1994.

Broadhead, J. L. "The 1999 Annual Award, the Foundation for the Malcolm Baldrige National Quality Award." [http://www.quality.nist.gov/law.htm]. 2000.

Browne, J. H. "Benchmarking HRM Practices in Healthy Work Organizations." *American Business Review,* June 2000, pp. 54–61.

Burt, R. S. "The Social Structure of Competition." In N. Nohria and R. G. Eccles (eds.), *Networks and Organizations: Structure, Form, and Action.* Boston: Harvard Business School Press, 1992.

Camp, R. C. *Benchmarking: The Search for Industry Best Practices That Lead to Superior Performance.* Milwaukee, Wis.: American Society for Quality Control Press, 1989.

Camp, R. C. *Business Process Benchmarking: Finding and Implementing Best Practices.* Milwaukee, Wis.: American Society for Quality Control Press, 1995.

Carnegie Foundation for the Advancement of Teaching. *National Survey on the Reexamination of Faculty Roles and Rewards.* Princeton, N.J.: Carnegie Foundation for the Advancement of Teaching, 1994.

Cox, J. R., Mann, L., and Samson, D. "Benchmarking as a Mixed Metaphor: Disentangling Assumptions of Competition and Collaboration." *Journal of Management Studies,* 1997, *34,* 285–314.

Danowski, J. A. "A Network-Based Content Analysis Methodology for Computer Mediated Communication: An Illustration with a Computer Bulletin Board." In M. Burgoon (ed.), *Communication Yearbook 6.* New Brunswick, N.J.: Transaction, 1982.

DeVito, D., and Morrison, S. "Benchmarking: A Tool for Sharing and Cooperation." *Journal for Quality and Participation,* Fall 2000, pp. 56–61.

Dewan, N. A., Daniels, A., Zieman, G., and Kramer, T. "The National Outcomes Management Project: A Benchmarking Collaborative." *Journal of Behavioral Health Services and Research,* 2000, *27,* 431–436.

DiMaggio, P. J., and Powell, W. W. "The Iron Cage Revisited: Institutional Isomorphism and Collective Rationality in Organizational Fields." *American Sociological Review,* 1983, *48,* 147–160.

Doerfel, M. L. "What Constitutes Semantic Network Analysis? A Comparison of Research and Methodologies." *Connections,* 1998, *21,* 16–26.

Doerfel, M. L., and Barnett, G. A. "A Semantic Network Analysis of the International Communication Association." *Human Communication Research,* 1999, *25,* 589–603.

Dopuch, N., and Gupta, M. "Estimation of Benchmarking Performance Standards: An Application to Public School Expenditures." *Journal of Accounting and Economics,* 1997, *23,* 141–161.

Elnathan, D., and Kim, O. "Partner Selection and Group Formation in Cooperative Benchmarking." *Journal of Accounting and Economics,* 1995, *19,* 345–364.

Euske, N. A., and Roberts, K. H. "Evolving Perspectives in Organization Theory: Communication Implications." In F. M. Jablin, L. L. Putnam, K. H. Roberts, and L. W. Porter (eds.), *Handbook of Organizational Communication: An Interdisciplinary Perspective.* Thousand Oaks, Calif.: Sage, 1987.

Feeley, T. H., and Barnett, G. A. "Predicting from Communication Networks." *Human Communication Research,* 1997, *23,* 370–387.

Fine, C. H. "Clockspeed-Based Strategies for Supply Chain Design." *Production and Operations Management,* 2000, *9,* 213–221.

Fitz-enz, J. "The Truth About 'Best Practice.'" *Human Resource Planning,* 1993, *16,* 19–26.

Freeman, C. A., and Barnett, G. A. "An Alternative Approach to Using Interpretive Theory to Examine Corporate Messages and Organizational Culture." In L. Thayer and G. A. Barnett (eds.), *Organization—Communication: Emerging Perspectives.* Vol. 4. Norwood, N.J.: Ablex, 1994.

Galaskiewicz, J. "The Structure of Community Organizational Networks." *Social Forces,* 1979, *57,* 1346–1363.

Glanz, E. E., and Daily, L. K. "Benchmarking." *Human Resource Management,* 1992, *31,* 9–20.

Jackson, N., and Lund, H. (eds.). *Benchmarking for Higher Education.* Buckingham, England: Society for Research into Higher Education and Open University Press, 2000.

Jarrar, Y. F., and Zairi, M. "Best Practice Transfer for Future Competitiveness: A Study of Best Practices." *Total Quality Management,* 2000, *11,* 734–740.

Johnson, R., and Seymour, D. "The Baldrige as an Award and Assessment Instrument for Higher Education." In D. Seymour (ed.), *High Performing Colleges I: Theory and Concepts.* Maryville, Mo.: Prescott, 1996.

Kaplan, R. S., and Norton, D. P. "The Balanced Scorecard—Measures That Drive Performance." *Harvard Business Review,* Jan.–Feb. 1992, pp. 71–79.

Kaplan, R. S., and Norton, D. P. "Putting the Balanced Scorecard to Work." *Harvard Business Review,* Sept.–Oct. 1993, pp. 134–142.

Kaplan, R. S., and Norton, D. P. *The Balanced Scorecard.* Boston: Harvard Business School Press, 1996.

Krackhardt, D. R., and Porter, L. W. "The Snowball Effect: Turnover Embedded in Social Networks." *Journal of Applied Psychology,* 1986, *71,* 50–55.

Lehr, J., and Ruben, B. D. "Excellence in Higher Education: A Baldrige-Based Self-Assessment Guide for Higher Education." *Assessment Update,* 1999, *11,* 1–4.

Lievrouw, L. A., Rogers, E. M., Lowe, C. U., and Nadel, E. "Triangulation as a Research Strategy for Identifying Invisible Colleges Among Biomedical Scientists." *Social Networks,* 1987, *9,* 217–248.

Longnecker, C., Stansfield, O., and Dwyer, T. C. "The Human Side of Manufacturing Improvement." *Business Horizons,* 1997, *40,* 7–17.

Manev, I. M., and Stevenson, W. B. "Balancing Ties: Boundary Spanning and Influence in the Organization's Extended Network of Communication." *Journal of Business Communication,* 2001, *38,* 183–205.

Martin, B. "Knowledge Management Within the Context of Management: An Evolving Relationship." *Singapore Management Review,* 2000, *22,* 17–37.

Miles, R. E., and Snow, C. C. "Organization: New Concepts for New Forms." *California Management Review,* 1986, *28,* 62–73.

Miles, R. E., and Snow, C. C. "Causes of Failure in Network Organizations." *California Management Review,* 1992, *34,* 53–70.

Monge, P. R., and Eisenberg, E. M. "Emergent Communication Networks." In F. Jablin, L. Putnam, K. Roberts, and L. Porter, (eds.), *Handbook of Organizational and Management Communication.* Thousand Oaks, Calif.: Sage, 1987.

Monge, P. R., and Fulk, J. "Communication Technology for Global Network Organizations." In G. DeSanctis and J. Fulk (eds.), *Shaping Organization Form: Communication, Connection, and Community.* Thousand Oaks, Calif.: Sage, 1999.

Morling, P., and Tanner, S. "Benchmarking a Public Service Business Management System." *Total Quality Management,* 2000, *11,* 417–426.

National Institute of Standards and Technology. "The 2000 Criteria for Performance Excellence for Business." [www.quality.nist.gov/qnew.htm]. 2000a.

National Institute of Standards and Technology. "The 2000 Criteria for Performance Excellence for Education." [www.quality.nist.gov/qnew.htm]. 2000b.

National Institute of Standards and Technology. "Frequently Asked Questions and Answers About the Malcolm Baldrige National Quality Award." [www.nist.gov/public__affairs/factsheet/baldfaqs.htm]. 2002.

Nohria, N., and Eccles, R. G. (eds.). *Networks and Organizations: Structure, Form, and Action.* Boston: Harvard Business School Press, 1992.

Pfeffer, J. *Competitive Advantage Through People.* Boston: Harvard Business School Press, 1994.

Pfeffer, J., and Salancik, G. R. *The External Control of Organizations: A Resource Dependence Perspective.* New York: HarperCollins, 1978.

Rice, R. E., and Danowski, J. A. "Is It Really Just Like a Fancy Answering Machine? Comparing Semantic Networks of Different Types of Voice Mail Users." *Journal of Business Communication,* 1993, *30,* 369–397.

Rigby, D. "Management Tools and Techniques: A Survey." *California Management Review,* 2001, *43,* 139–160.

Ruben, B. D. *Excellence in Higher Education 2001–2002: A Baldrige-Based Guide to Organizational Assessment, Planning and Improvement.* Washington, D.C.: National Association of College and University Business Officers, 2001.

Ruben, B. D., and Sandmeyer, L. E. "NCCI's Role in Higher Education." *Business Officer,* Aug. 2001, pp. 35–38.

Sanchez, J. I., Kraus, E., White, S., and Williams, M. "Adopting High Involvement Human Resources Practices: The Mediating Role of Benchmarking." *Group and Organization Management,* 1999, *24,* 461–478.

Schuler, R. S. *Managing Human Resources.* (6th ed.) Cincinnati, Ohio: South-Western College Publications, 1998.

Shoham, A., and Fiegenbaum, A. "Extending the Competitive Marketing Strategy Paradigm: The Role of Strategic Reference Points Theory." *Journal of the Academy of Marketing Science,* 1999, *27,* 442–454.

Susskind, A. M., Miller, V. D., and Johnson, J. D. "Downsizing and Structural Holes: Their Impact on Layoff Survivors' Perceptions of Organizational Chaos and Openness to Change." *Communication Research,* 1998, *25,* 30–65.

Taylor, F. W. *The Principles of Scientific Management.* New York: HarperCollins, 1911.

Terziovski, M., Sohal, A., and Moss, S. "Longitudinal Analysis of Quality Management Practices in Australian Organizations." *Total Quality Management,* 1999, *10,* 915–926.

Trout, P. A. "What the Numbers Mean." *Change,* Sept.–Oct. 1997, pp. 25–30.

Troutt, M. D., Gribbin, D. W., Shanker, M., and Zhang, A. "Cost Efficiency Benchmarking for Operational Units with Multiple Cost Drivers." *Decision Sciences*, 2000, *31*, 813–832.

Ulijn, J., O'Hair, D., Weggeman, M., Ledlow, G., and Hall, H. T. "Innovation, Corporate Strategy, and Cultural Context: What Is the Mission for International Business Communication?" *Journal of Business Communication*, 2000, *37*, 293–317.

Upcraft, M. L., and Schuh, J. H. (eds.). *Assessment in Student Affairs: A Guide for Practitioners.* San Francisco: Jossey-Bass, 1996.

Voss, B. "At Witt's End." *Journal of Business Strategy*, 1993, *14*(5) 38–39.

Weber, M. *The Theory of Social and Economic Organization.* New York: Free Press, 1947.

Williams, W. M., and Ceci, J. J. "How'm I Doing? Problems with Student Ratings of Instructors and Courses." *Change*, Sept.-Oct. 1997, pp. 12–23.

Yarrow, D. J., and Prabhu, V. B. "Collaborating to Compete: Benchmarking Through Regional Partnerships." *Total Quality Management*, 1999, *10*, 793–802.

Zairi, M. *Competitive Benchmarking—An Executive Guide.* Letchworth, England: Technical Communications Publishing, 1992.

MARYA L. DOERFEL is assistant professor of communication at Rutgers University.

BRENT D. RUBEN is distinguished professor of communication and executive director of Rutgers CQI at Rutgers University.

2

This chapter discusses the Integrated Postsecondary Education Data System as a tool for collecting data to be used in benchmarking studies.

The Integrated Postsecondary Education Data System

John H. Schuh

The demand for accountability in higher education has been growing for many years (Borden and Banta, 1994). "National governments, state and provincial legislatures, boards of trustees, and professional accrediting agencies are calling for concrete evidence that institutions of higher education are worth the large public and private investments they receive" (Borden and Bottrill, 1994, p. 5). In response to these pressures, college and university administrators have developed various methodologies including benchmarks (Spendolini, 1992), strategic indicators (Taylor and Massy, 1996), and performance indicators (Banta and Borden, 1994), to demonstrate the extent to which their institutions are meeting their goals. All of these measures can improve organizational performance (Marchese, 1997), compare an institution's performance against those of other institutions (Miller, 1997), or contrast an institution of higher education with organizations in other enterprises (Rush, 1994).

While the methods that institutions develop and implement to demonstrate their accountability vary widely, all effective programs should include the collection and interpretation of reliable data. When governing boards ask administrators to provide comparative data on room and board rates for similar colleges in the region, for example, the administrators could make numerous telephone calls to colleagues at peer institutions; develop, distribute, and collect questionnaires; or spend an extensive amount of time searching the World Wide Web. While these approaches may once have been the best methods for gathering comparative data, the Integrated Postsecondary Education Data System (IPEDS) provides a more readily accessible and comprehensive approach to accessing institutional data for benchmarking with appropriate institutional peer groups than other methods of data collection.

IPEDS is a comprehensive federal database that includes enormous amounts of information about higher education institutions in the United States. When it's used appropriately, IPEDS can provide administrators with a wealth of data to help influence their decisions. This chapter will discuss the IPEDS system, provide an example of how it can be used in benchmarking, identify several projects that have been completed using IPEDS, and describe its strengths and weaknesses. Those who are interested in using IPEDS are encouraged to access the Web site at nces.ed.gov/ipeds.

IPEDS Overview

"The IPEDS is a system of surveys that collects data from all institutions in the U.S. whose primary mission is to provide postsecondary education" (Peng and Korb, 1989, p. 78) and is available to anyone with a fairly powerful computer who has access to the Web. IPEDS is managed by the United States Department of Education, National Center for Education Statistics (NCES). Data are collected on a periodic basis from postsecondary institutions through a variety of survey instruments that are available at the IPEDS home page. For those who are interested in learning more about the substance of the questions in the surveys, as well as the definitions NCES uses in crafting its data sets, links are provided for each questionnaire used in building the system.

The IPEDS database is in the public domain, so anyone can access the information without obtaining permission. One should, however, use appropriate referencing in publishing data from the system. About the only limit for studies using the IPEDS system are the creativity and ingenuity of the investigator, although the sophistication of data analysis provided by the IPEDS system is limited.

The IPEDS home page lets visitors learn about the site, study a publications list, and review survey forms. A link also is available to the peer-analysis system, which includes a tutorial recommended for first-time users.

Because one of the purposes of IPEDS is to conduct peer comparisons, investigators will need to know the six-digit number of the institution that is the focus of the study. Without this number, investigators can't access the appropriate level of data, which will provide the most accurate information. Investigators can find this number on the IPEDS home page link to College Opportunities On-Line (COOL). COOL provides hot links to virtually every institution in the country.

Determining a Comparison Group

The size of the database lets investigators identify a tremendous combination of variables when they're creating a peer group of institutions for benchmarking purposes. The Web site has a peer group feature that automatically creates a list of institutions to include for comparison purposes. It is not entirely clear, however, how the peer group is identified. For Iowa State University, a state-assisted, doctoral-extensive, land grant institution, the automatic peer group function provided eight universities:

- University of Iowa
- University of Kansas
- Kansas State University
- University of Minnesota–Twin Cities
- University of Missouri–Columbia
- Saint Louis University
- Washington University (St. Louis)
- University of Nebraska–Lincoln

While this set is not entirely flawed, in this group of peers are two private universities and four that are not land grant institutions. Still, if one is just beginning an inquiry and has no reference point regarding which institutions to consider as peers for benchmarking purposes, the automatic peer group function is an efficient and effective place to start. However, investigators can access a number of variables, shown in Exhibit 2.1, through the relational database.

These variables give the investigator a wide range of options for defining a peer group. For example, the Carnegie classification code variable provides all of the classifications of the old Carnegie system—Research I, Research II, Doctoral I, and so on. Simply by selecting the desired classification, such as Research II, the investigator can call up a list of all similar institutions in the IPEDS system. By adding variables, such as Control of Institution (Public or Private) and region of the country, for example, the investigator can refine the peer group to include all public Research II universities or all private Research II universities located in a specific region such as the Southwest.

The variables for selecting a peer group are extensive: even data pertaining to athletic conferences are available. The scope of conference information is broad and includes data from NCAA Division I conferences, such as the Atlantic Coast Conference, to those that are regional in nature, such as the Wisconsin Intercollegiate Athletic Conference. The only limit to choosing a comparison group is that the database can handle a maximum of seven hundred institutions for any given inquiry. The database could not handle all community colleges in the United States, for example, as the total number of community colleges in the United States exceeds seven hundred.

An example of a straightforward inquiry would be the identification of the public Research I institutions that have the twenty lowest mandatory tuition and fee charges for in-state students for the most recent available year. To do so, the investigator would have to select as characteristics the Carnegie classification and the sources of institutional control. After choosing these variables, the investigator would select "Research I" and "public"

Exhibit 2.1. Comparison Group Variable in the IPEDS Relational Database

Relational Database
Post office state abbreviation code
FIPS state code
OBE region code
Employer identification number
Dunn and Bradstreet identification number
Office of Postsecondary Education ID
OPE eligibility code
Sector of institution
Level of institution
Control of institution
Affiliation of institution
Highest level of offering
Undergraduate offering
Graduate offering
First-professional offering
Highest degree offered
Degree granting status
Percent black, non-Hispanic
Percent American Indiana/Alaskan Native
Percent Asian/Pacific Islander
Percent Hispanic
Historically black college or university
Institution has hospital
Institution grants a medical degree
Tribal college
Carnegie Classification Code
Degree of urbanization
Institution open to the general public
Status of institution
Institution is active in current year

as the defining characteristics. The yield is a total of fifty-eight institutions, not including the original institution, which, in this example, is the University of Michigan.

Accessing and Analyzing Data

Once the investigator has defined the comparison group, the next step is to access the data. Again, huge amounts of data are available, including eight comprehensive categories with multiple subcategories that include many specific variables. Longitudinal data also are available in many of the categories from 1995 through 1999 or 2000; see Table 2.1 for a list of categories and years available at the time of this writing. Investigators need to remember that the years listed on the chart are survey years—the year when the data were collected. When reporting results, it is imperative that the data be cited as being from the survey year.

Table 2.1. Data Sets Available

Category	Years
Institutional characteristics	1990, 1995, 1997, 1998, 1999, 2000
Fall enrollments	1990, 1995, 1997, 1998, 1999
Postsecondary completions	1990, 1995, 1997, 1998, 1999, 2000
Faculty salaries	1990, 1995, 1997, 1998, 1999
Fall staff	1995, 1997, 1999
Finance	1990, 1995, 1997, 1998, 1999
IPSFA survey	1997
Graduation rates	1997

Those accessing the site can follow the prompts to the appropriate tuition and fee charges. The display that lists these costs of attendance provides a wide range of choices related to tuition for undergraduate and graduate students for academic year programs (see Exhibit 2.2). For the example, we would choose (1) Tuition FTFY UG in-state and (2) in-state undergraduate required fees. This is a little complicated because the data are located in two files. The data can be accessed quite easily, however, then incorporated into a spreadsheet program for analysis.

The IPEDS relational database lets investigators compute basic statistics and other simple manipulations of data such as developing measures of central tendency. As shown in Table 2.2, the data have been transferred to an Excel spreadsheet, which provides the opportunity to study the information in more depth. Institutions can be ranked within the specific category based on where they place in their peer group.

Many studies have been conducted using IPEDS. Because the database has such a wealth of data, the topics of these studies vary widely. Examples of these studies include a report on endowment spending at private colleges (Basch, 1999), African American and white students' degree expectations (Carter, 1999), and administrative satisfaction with the governmental regulatory climate in the 1990s (Volkwein, Malik, and Napierski-Pranci, 1998). As the topics of these studies demonstrate, the use of the database has a wide variety of applications for institutional research in higher education.

Advantages and Disadvantages of IPEDS

The IPEDS relational data base has a number of strengths and weaknesses of which the user should be aware.

Advantages. One of the strengths of the IPEDS system is that every institution in the United States is required to provide information whenever questionnaires are submitted to them. As a consequence, an investigator can identify a wide range of institutions for comparison purposes. For example, an institution located on the East Coast could compare itself along certain dimensions (room and board charges, tuition and fees, headcount enrollment, and number of full-time faculty) with institutions located on the East

Exhibit 2.2. Tuition and Fee Categories for Undergraduate and Graduate Students (Academic Year Programs) Listed in the IPEDS Relational Database

Tuition FTFY undergraduate in-district
In-district undergraduate required fees
In-district undergraduate per credit hour charge
In-district undergraduate comprehensive fee
Tuition FTFY undergraduate in-state
In-state undergraduate required fees
In-state undergraduate per credit hour fees
In-state undergraduate comprehensive fees
Tuition FTFY undergraduate out-of-state
Out-of-state undergraduate per credit hour charge
Out-of-state undergraduate comprehensive fees
Tuition FTFY graduate in-district
In-district graduate required fees
In-district graduate per credit hour charge
Tuition FTFY graduate in-state
In-state graduate required fees
In-state graduate per credit hour charge
Tuition FTFY graduate out-of-state
Out-of-state graduate required fees
Out-of-state graduate per credit hour charge
Institution has hospital
Institution grants a medical degree
Tribal college
Carnegie Classification Code
Degree of Urbanization
Institution open to the general public
Status of institution
Institution is active in current year

and West coasts. By developing a peer group of institutions on each coast, the project could be completed using IPEDS. This inquiry presumably would be significantly more time consuming if the project were done without IPEDS: it would require extensive staff time to identify the initial set of peer institutions, let alone secure the specific data that were being sought.

Because the database has such a large number of institutional variables that can be incorporated into a peer group (see Exhibit 2.1), virtually an infinite number of variables can be included in developing a peer group. This allows for great specificity in identifying a peer group, a feature that may not be possible if one is to rely simply on geography, Carnegie type, or some other distinctive factor in determining a peer group. In short, one can identify "peer institutions, competitors or industry leaders" (Peng and Korb, 1989, p. 80) quite easily by using IPEDS. At a specific institution, decision makers or planners can identify those aspects of the institutions that are most salient for comparison purposes, then find a group of institutions that

Table 2.2. IPEDS Ranking of Lowest 20 Research 1 Universities by In-State Tuition and Fee Charges

| | Mandatory | | |
University	Tuition	Fees	Total
University of Tennessee (Knoxville)	$2,812	$550	$3,362
Georgia Institute of Technology	$2,506	$802	$3,308
University of Georgia	$2,506	$770	$3,276
University of Iowa	$2,906	$298	$3,204
University of Colorado	$2,514	$674	$3,188
University of Hawaii	$3,024	$133	$3,157
Colorado State University	$2,408	$725	$3,133
Iowa State University	$2,906	$226	$3,132
University of Utah	$2,371	$526	$2,897
University of West Virginia	$1,332	$1,504	$2,836
University of New Mexico	$2,259	$536	$2,795
New Mexico State University	$1,956	$834	$2,790
North Carolina State University	$1,806	$954	$2,760
University of Kansas	$2,267	$458	$2,725
University of North Carolina (Chapel Hill)	$1,860	$850	$2,710
Utah State University	$1,947	$456	$2,403
Florida State University	$1,554	$824	$2,378
University of Arizona	$2,348	$0	$2,348
Arizona State University	$2,272	$74	$2,346
University of Florida	$1,540	$702	$2,242

Source: IPEDS Relational Data Base, 2000 Survey Year.

Note: University of Arizona is listed as reporting tuition and fees together.

meet the identified criteria. Depending on what is to be compared, a variety of comparison groups could be identified to meet the specific informational needs of the project.

One of the most difficult problems in questionnaire construction—developing an instrument that is understood and interpreted similarly by all respondents—becomes less of an issue in the questionnaires used to build the IPEDS database because the same definitions are used in multiple data collections. Rather than having to create a questionnaire for a specific project using definitions that may not be universally understood, the investigator can rely on the definitions used by the IPEDS instruments, thereby enhancing the accuracy of the data.

As mentioned above, participation in the periodic institutional IPEDS surveys is not optional. Consequently, fairly complete sets of data are available for the various areas of inquiry explored by these questionnaires. Not all institutions complete every item for every questionnaire, however. But when one compares the completion rate of IPEDS surveys with individually prepared questionnaires, the difference is dramatic. Moreover, the material is provided by individuals who have access to appropriate institutional databases. A thorny problem for many research projects is identifying the person on an individual campus who is in the best position to provide the most accurate information to a questionnaire. This is not a problem for the investigator using IPEDS.

The speed with which a project can be completed using IPEDS is a great strength of the database. Because the data are readily available, all the investigator has to do is to access the Web site and begin work. The alternative, collecting data by mail or even using electronic mail, can take a much longer period of time. When time is of the essence, it is very difficult to find a quicker way to access information than through the IPEDS system.

The IPEDS system allows for great flexibility in conducting an inquiry. Rather than relying on a database that might overlook certain areas of investigation, the IPEDS system provides a wealth of information that can be manipulated to meet specific institutional needs. For example, suppose an institution wanted to calculate the percentage of faculty who are tenured or on tenure track and then compare this percentage with a peer group. It could look at how its percentage compares with similar institutions by geography, control (public or private), Carnegie type, housing capacity, or some other measure. With a couple of keystrokes, the comparison could be completed.

Finally, the longitudinal data that are available in the IPEDS system can be extremely valuable for tracking patterns and trends over time. "Analyzing longitudinal data has enabled researchers to provide meaningful descriptions of change over time, and to explore causal relationships of two or more factors interacting at several points of time" (Pavel and Reiser, 1991, p. 6). To study a problem for a specific year is useful, but to put it in the context of a longer period of time can be very helpful in determining if the issue is an anomaly or part of a long-term trend.

Disadvantages. Several disadvantages are associated with using the IPEDS database. The categories available in the database are quite broad, and do not allow for precision in identifying specific programs or initiatives. For example, expenditure categories in the financial aspects of the system are very general. These include such categories as student services, instruction, and physical plant. Categories that are more specific are not available. In student affairs, for example, one cannot determine how much was spent on career services, student activities, or counseling services. IPEDS, therefore, cannot satisfy a query to make more narrow comparisons across expenditure categories.

The only computations that are available are measures of central tendency, rankings, and so on. Any more sophisticated analysis has to be made by exporting the data to a Statistical Package for the Social Sciences (SPSS) computer program. If one wanted, for example, to examine the correlation between institutional type and tuition and fee charges, the IPEDS database could provide the raw data, but the analysis would have to be computed using another statistical program.

Finally, the data reported in the survey year could be confusing. The IPEDS data collection process is complex, and sometimes the year refers to the fiscal year, while at other times it refers to the academic year (Barbett, personal communication, February 26, 2001). As a consequence, the best way to report the data is by Survey year, as that reflects the year that data were published in the database.

Conclusion

The Integrated Post Secondary Data System provides quick, easy access to a large database that can provide information for benchmarking projects. From a national perspective, it provides a wealth of data that can help quantify and describe the status of specific aspects of higher education, thereby helping influence decisions pertaining to national priorities in postsecondary education. At the institutional level, IPEDS data can be manipulated to develop a wide range of peer groups that form the basis for cross-institutional comparisons. Knowledgeable use of IPEDS, including an understanding of its strengths and limitations, can assist investigators in more fully understanding their institutions and how they compare with their peers.

References

Banta, T. W., and Borden, V.M.H. "Performance Indicators for Accountability and Improvement." In V.M.H. Borden and T. W. Banta (eds.), *Using Performance Indicators to Guide Strategic Decision Making*. New Directions for Institutional Research, no. 82. San Francisco: Jossey-Bass, 1994.

Basch, D. L. "Changes in the Endowment Spending of Private Colleges in the Early 1990s." *Journal of Higher Education*, 1999, *70*, 278–308.

Borden, V.M.H., and Banta, T. W. "Editors' Notes." In V.M.H. Borden and T. W. Banta (eds.), *Using Performance Indicators to Guide Strategic Decision Making*. New Directions for Institutional Research, no. 82. San Francisco: Jossey-Bass, 1994.

Borden, V.M.H., and Bottrill, K. V. "Performance Indicators: History, Definitions, and Methods." In V.M.H. Borden and T. W. Banta (eds.), *Using Performance Indicators to Guide Strategic Decision Making*. New Directions for Institutional Research, no. 82. San Francisco: Jossey-Bass, 1994.

Carter, D. F. "The Impact of Institutional Choice and Environments on African-American and White Students' Degree Expectations." *Research in Higher Education*, 1999, *40*, 17–41.

Marchese, T. J. "Sustaining Quality Enhancement in Academic and Managerial Life." In M. W. Peterson, D. D. Dill, L. A. Mets, and Associates, *Planning and Management for a Changing Environment*. San Francisco: Jossey-Bass, 1997.

Miller, T. K. "Benchmarking: Comparing Performance Across Organizations." In M. L. Upcraft and J. H. Schuh (eds.), *Assessment in Student Affairs*. San Francisco: Jossey-Bass, 1997.

Pavel, D. M., and Reiser, M. "Using National Data Bases to Examine Minority Student Success in Higher Education." In C. S. Lenth (ed.), *Using National Data Bases*. New Directions for Institutional Research, no. 69. San Francisco: Jossey-Bass, 1991.

Peng, S. S., and Korb, R. A. "Using National Data Bases in Analyzing the Institutional Impacts of Student Aid." In R. H. Fenske (ed.), *Studying the Impact of Student Aid on Institutions*. New Directions for Institutional Research, no. 62. San Francisco: Jossey-Bass, 1989.

Rush, S. C. "Benchmarking—How Good is Good?" In W. F. Massy and J. W. Meyerson (eds.), *Measuring Institutional Performance in Higher Education*. Princeton, N.J.: Peterson's, 1994.

Spendolini, M. J. *The Benchmarking Book*. New York: American Management Association, 1992.

Taylor, B. E., and Massy, W. F. *Strategic Indicators for Higher Education*. Princeton, N.J.: Peterson's, 1996.

Volkwein, J. F., Malik, S. M., and Napierski-Pranci, M. *Research in Higher Education*, 1998, *39*, 43–63.

JOHN H. SCHUH is professor and chair of educational leadership and policy studies at Iowa State University. He was a fellow at the National Center for Education Statistics in summer 2000.

3

This chapter examines how benchmarking can be used to assist in making decisions about tuition and fees. Emphasis is placed on generating sufficient tuition income to fund institutional operations.

Using Benchmarking to Influence Tuition and Fee Decisions

Loren W. Loomis Hubbell, Robert J. Massa, Lucie Lapovsky

All but a handful of independent colleges and universities are dependent on tuition and fee income to finance the bulk of their operating budgets. Thus the management of tuition rates, tuition revenue (net and gross), financial aid strategy, and enrollment is critical to an institution's financial health. This chapter explores the drivers underlying this critical revenue source, the relationship of net revenue to expenditures, the relationship between enrollment and costs, and the contributions of effective benchmarking to institutional decision-making processes.

Tuition discounting, which is designed to maximize enrollment as well as net revenue, became more common in the 1990s. The simple theory is that by offering a discount to selected students, enrollments could be increased to capacity. It is critical that an institution define its capacity both in terms of potential and the institution's current capacity. Capacity relates to both human and physical resources.

Discounting was originally designed to help provide access for those with insufficient financial resources and to help create a diversified campus environment. Over time, these goals became intertwined with institutional capacity, enrollment management, and revenue generation. Now, there are very few schools in which financial aid is managed with the single purpose of economic diversity and many in which it is a centerpiece of year-to-year net revenue management. Without discounts applied in a strategic way, many institutions would be under-enrolled and thus forgo revenue.

What happened, of course, is that discounting became a competitive tool as well as a means to maximize revenues. Institutions employed discounting strategies to affect not only revenue, but also—in competing

NEW DIRECTIONS FOR HIGHER EDUCATION, no. 118, Summer 2002 © Wiley Periodicals, Inc.

against peers for the best students at the optimal price—the composition and quality of students.

The complex and dynamic relationships between tuition rates, enrollment patterns, institutional capacity, and financial aid strategy together form the drivers behind net tuition revenue. In the final analysis, it is net, not gross, tuition revenue that provides the funds for educational services and institutional infrastructure. Thus we will look more closely at these drivers, to consider what benchmarks might best help us understand their relevance to our institutions and to apply them to our decision making.

Background

It helps to look at the history of net and gross pricing and to understand how the industry came to its current pricing structure of increasingly meaningless sticker prices and significant discounts. Prior to the era of strategic discounting, from the 1960s through most of the 1980s, a reduction in tuition was given primarily in the form of need-based financial aid. For most of that time, there was either a national standard for determining need established by the College Scholarship Service or a Congressional needs analysis formula which was uniformly accepted. Any variance of expected contributions from families among different institutions was minimal.

All this began to change in 1990 when the Justice Department began to investigate more than sixty institutions for antitrust violations in sharing aid data and agreeing on family contribution figures. The investigation resulted in the abandonment of college "overlap groups" (groups of institutions that often received applications from the same students and shared information about applicants). It also indirectly led to the formulation of a federal methodology in 1992 that allowed institutions great leeway in determining eligibility for institutional aid between the federal eligibility floor and the more restrictive uniform or Congressional needs test previously employed. Since that time, institutions have used financial aid to maximize a competitive advantage, often applying different needs tests to different groups of students and more frequently distributing institutional gift aid on a merit basis. Merit, or the broader descriptive term, *non-need-based aid*, with the concomitant use of differential needs analysis formulas, has become a euphemism for strategic financial aid leveraging, or discounting.

Discounting

This said, discounting is not a practice of using aid for non-need-based awards. Discounting is the practice of providing reduced net price, for whatever institutional goal and to whomever it is offered, regardless of the criteria chosen for its administration. It is not a new, sneaky practice to aid the rich and cheat the poor. It is, when well designed, a strategy to manage the composition of the student body and increase revenue while remaining true to institutional mission and objectives. Badly designed—in commission or omission—it threatens an institution's major source of revenue and its bottom line. The worst-case scenario occurs when enrollment decreases, financial aid increases, and instructional and other institutional operating costs increase, often plunging an institution into a financial deficit.

Strategic use of discounting amounts to leveraging. Leveraging, as it is practiced in colleges and universities, awards just the right amount of aid or discount to enroll a particular student and, in the aggregate, just the right amount of aid to enroll a class of a planned size with specific characteristics. There are many systems, from simple to complex, to do this. At the most arithmetically sophisticated level, regression formulas that combine data on groups of students from previous years are used to predict the enrollment behavior of prospective students. They are based, in part, on variations of the grant (or discount) awarded. This is a major departure from straight, need-based financial aid, but it is a subject for another discussion, concerning the decline in access to higher education for students from lower-income backgrounds—a serious issue for American higher education today.

In the 1990s, discount rates at independent colleges climbed from roughly 29 percent in the fall of 1991 to almost 38 percent in the fall of 2000 (Lapovsky and Loomis Hubbell, 2001). This means that institutions, on average, retain only 62 cents of each tuition dollar, down from 71 cents a decade ago. Without other sources of revenue to compensate for this loss, discounts may limit the ability of institutions to fund programs, salaries, and facilities.

Institutions with unfilled enrollment capacity, however, can use strategic discounting to increase enrollments and net revenue. It may be better, for example, to offer a space to a qualified student at a discounted price than to have that space go unfilled, forgoing all revenue and underusing faculty resources and facilities. It is essential, though, to offer those discounts only to students who would not enroll at a higher price. To do otherwise risks net revenue loss. Alternatively, if the college is already at capacity, increasing enrollment whether with full pay or discounted students may not be advantageous and certainly will be harmful to the school's finances, especially if the students are heavily discounted.

The trend in discounting has led to a growth in the consultant industry, with many companies large and small promising to help institutions maximize enrollment goals and net tuition revenue through the use of leveraged discounting. Of course, the problem is that discounting escalates each year as colleges compete against one another for the best students. Further complicating management's work, student enrollment behavior in one year often does not, in a dynamic environment, predict behavior in the next.

One way to get a handle on institutional tuition and fee policy, including the use of discounts, is through careful benchmarking. Using the fictional Guilder College, this chapter will describe a paradigm of benchmarking from the *macro* (total revenue, revenue composition, and total costs) to the *micro* (net tuition revenue, discount rate, discounting strategies, and cost per student) using four types of benchmarking: industry, internal, peer, best in class (Alstete, 1995).

But if individual enrollment behaviors depend on external environmental issues (the economy, what the competition is doing) as well as on the perception of institutional value and market position, will benchmarking, as a means to assess institutional practices and outcomes, be subject to the same criticism as leveraging formulas used to maximize enrollments and revenue? Certainly—in combination with an understanding of the enrollment behaviors of our prospective students, benchmarking conducted at regular intervals will help institutions gauge their experiences against others and will allow a strategic assessment of institutional practices and policies.

Guilder College

Guilder is a small private college with a traditional-age undergraduate student body. For most of the 1990s, Guilder could benchmark itself to national industry standards in the "small college, high tuition" category. During that time, Guilder experienced significant enrollment pressures. It experimented with holding tuition flat from fiscal year 1996 through fiscal year 1998 to impact enrollment and net revenue, but that strategy failed to produce the desired outcome: it resulted in a lower net tuition revenue and only a marginal gain in enrollment. Fortunately for Guilder, concurrent to the pressures in enrollment and net tuition revenue, the college achieved some success in a capital campaign and a generally increasing market in the late 1990s, posting 12 percent to 14 percent gains in endowment spending each year from fiscal year 1998 to fiscal year 2001. This was not enough, however, to offset a significant decline in net tuition revenue of 37 percent from fiscal year 1995 to fiscal year 1998. Facing truly serious financial difficulty, Guilder took the bold step of dropping its tuition rate in fiscal year 1999 by almost 30 percent. Net tuition revenue slowly began to climb as a result in fiscal year 2000 and fiscal year 2001, as did enrollments.

Once Guilder reduced its tuition, it shifted its national industry standard group to the "small college, low tuition" category. To define its position among peers, it identified two similar institutions: Peer 1, which is also considered to be "best in class," and Peer 2, which tracked more closely to Guilder in enrollment but behind Guilder in net tuition revenue per student, until fiscal year 1999, when it experienced a significant jump in freshman enrollment and net tuition revenue after employing an aggressive discounting strategy and some realignment of its programs and marketing.

Source Data

Relevant data for all three institutions is included in several tables throughout the chapter. The data were derived from a number of sources. (Guilder and its peers are completely fictional colleges.)

A number of good reference sources are available widely. A few are worth highlighting here. Good sources for industry data on tuition and aid, including overall revenue composition benchmarks, include

- Original source publications such as the *Digest of Education Statistics* from the National Center for Education Statistics, publications from the Bureau of Labor Statistics, the College Board's periodic and special reports based on the *Annual Survey of Colleges,* and the National Association of College and University Business Officers annual survey of tuition discounting
- Derivative analyses by industry veterans such as the Research Associates of Washington and Minter Associates
- Summaries from a variety of sources aggregated in the *Chronicle of Higher Education*'s annual *Almanac* issue
- Periodic monographs written by experts in the education industry

Good sources for peer information include releases from the National Center for Education Statistics of school-specific IPEDS data, repackaged (and easier to use) IPEDS data issued by Minter Associates and others, the telephone, and the Web. The latter two are particularly useful for the timely exchange of financial statements and other pertinent data, and for gaining an effective understanding of the underlying patterns. Regional and peer data sharing groups can also be very effective.

Total Revenue and Revenue Composition

Tuition revenue and financial aid decisions are part of an overall revenue picture for each institution. Whereas this chapter focuses on the role of gross and net tuition and using benchmarks to influence tuition and aid decisions, it is important to place tuition revenue in its institutional context.

Institutional revenues come from many sources. Private colleges and universities derive their revenues predominantly from tuition and other student sources such as housing, board, and bookstores. Other revenue sources include government and private grants, charitable donations, income from endowment and other investments, and other auxiliary or independent income sources. Some institutions add medical school and hospital revenues to this mix. Public institutions generally will have lower tuition revenues but will add substantive public support in the form of state and local appropriations.

Using Guilder as an example, questions we might ask in this context-setting exercise include the following:

- What is happening in the industry with regard to the role of tuition and other revenue sources?
- What have Guilder's trends been over this period?
- How does Guilder stand against its peer institutions?

Table 3.1. Private Colleges and Universities

	1994–95	1969–70	Compound Annual Growth
Tuition and fee revenue (in 000s)	$29,598,772	$2,684,848	
Student aid expenditures (in 000s)	$7,623,304	$527,617	
Net tuition and fee revenue (in 000s)	$21,975,468	$2,157,231	
Full instructional expenditures* (in 000s)	$34,294,000	$3,987,000	
Full-time equivalent enrollment	$2,583,141	$1,756,153	
Ratio of			
Tuition to full instructional expenditures	86%	67%	1.0%
Net tuition to full instructional expenditures	64%	54%	0.7%
Tuition and fee revenue per student	$11,458	$1,526	8.4%
Student aid expenditures per student	$2,951	$300	9.6%
Net tuition revenues per student	$8,507	$1,226	8.1%

Note: Full instructional expenditures include instruction, student services, academic and institutional support, plant operations, and maintenance, less estimated overhead cost recovery for research and public service, estimated at 30 percent of the expenditures for those two functions.

Source: Halstead, 1998, p. 50.

The goal in asking these questions is to use the benchmark information to assess the position of the college, in the context of both the industry and peer competitors, and with an eye toward managing overall revenue resources so there is a sustainable institutional balance among the various sources. Greater reliance on tuition and fee revenues means greater vulnerability to application counts, retention, and the combined effects of willingness and ability to pay. Greater reliance on endowment income and private philanthropy means greater vulnerability to economic shifts in the market, though institutions highly dependent on these sources tend to find them more reliable than revenues derived from the year-to-year decisions of seventeen- to twenty-three-year-olds. Higher endowment and private donation revenues are also positively correlated with greater overall institutional wealth; tuition and fee revenue is usually still a strong player in the revenue stream.

Statistics based on federal surveys tend not to be as timely as other sources of information, but they provide a truly comprehensive look at the higher education industry. As shown in Table 3.1, for private colleges and universities nationally, tuition and fee revenue has increasingly played a role in the revenue composition.

When we're comparing the core, or mission-central, expense of delivering instructional services in the 1969–70 and 1994–95 school years, we find that the tuition and fees increased from 67 percent to 86 percent of the funding source. Over this twenty-five-year period, tuition and fees covered on average 1 percent more of the costs of education each year. Conversely, other sources of revenue covered on average 1 percent less of these expenditures each year. Net tuition revenues increased more slowly over the twenty-five years (due to the explosive growth in aid over this period) rising from 54 percent to 64 percent of full instructional costs, a compound annual growth rate of 0.7 percent.

Guilder's experience, in recent years, however, has been rather different. In the 1994–95 school year, the ratio of net tuition revenue to full instructional expense was 51 percent, significantly less than the national average for that year. Over the intervening five years to 1999–00, the ratio dropped to 40 percent as Guilder's revenue composition tilted away from tuition revenue and toward endowment and private donation (see Table 3.2). From this benchmark, Guilder College's managers infer that their revenue balance is weighted to the more durable and generally more stable sources of endowment and charitable giving than generally would be true of the industry.

Though it may be reassuring to have the level of endowment and donation support enjoyed by Guilder, the college's leaders acknowledged that much of the shift had come from enrollment and discounting difficulties; only part of the shift was intentional fundraising. (This discovery underscores the need to look beyond prima facie interpretations of benchmarks!) The trend statistics shown in Table 3.2 reflect the sources of revenue as presented in Guilder's audited financial statements. They reveal all too clearly the difficulty the college has had in raising net tuition revenues, though the reduction in tuition rates in 1998 and resultant financial aid impact has, after a terribly difficult first year, clearly helped. The statements also show the benefits of a significant capital campaign which has been realized in both capital and operational donation. These statistics on the percentage for the components of total revenue help frame the role of tuition in the total institutional picture of revenue sources and revenue sufficiency.

Finally, Guilder administrators looked at the components of revenue in their peer schools (see Figure 3.1). At Peer 1, net tuition revenues made up 52 percent of total operating revenues with auxiliaries at 30 percent, endowment at 10 percent, and private gifts and grants at 4 percent. Peer 2 had 46 percent of its operating revenues from net tuition with 33 percent coming from auxiliaries, 9 percent from endowment, and 6 percent from charitable giving.

Using these multiple benchmarks creates a framework for Guilder's overall revenue strategy and, within that strategy, the role of tuition and financial aid. The indicators show the weakness of the college's operating revenue stream over time. They also illustrate the opportunity it now has to leverage from the *de facto* rebalancing of the revenue side to manage all components to produce a strong revenue stream.

Tuition Revenue

Benchmarking tuition rates and enrollment is probably the most widely used benchmarking practice in college finance and admissions offices. Senior administrators often can tell you how their enrollments have

Table 3.2. Trends in Operating Revenues at Guilder

Guilder College Trends in Operating Revenues	1994–95	1995–96	1996–97	1997–98	1998–99	1999–00
Tuition and fee revenue	$16,694,441	$15,980,563	$15,913,998	$11,732,837	$12,610,712	$13,331,698
Less financial aid discount	$6,341,000	$6,684,005	$7,518,561	$5,226,607	$5,074,315	$5,193,055
Net tuition revenue	$10,353,441	$9,296,558	$8,395,437	$6,506,230	$7,536,397	$8,138,643
Auxiliary services	$4,234,552	$4,772,894	$5,027,846	$5,597,530	$6,726,578	$7,120,018
Government grants	$261,349	$256,311	$223,999	$259,777	$379,326	$344,038
Private gifts and grants	$3,104,420	$1,565,109	$1,856,283	$1,656,511	$1,795,761	$2,564,347
Endowment spending and other interest income	$1,848,456	$1,863,569	$2,135,816	$2,422,468	$2,545,265	$2,905,179
Other	$394,913	$412,728	$418,880	$578,352	$558,184	$547,855
Total operating revenues	$20,197,131	$18,167,169	$18,058,261	$17,020,908	$19,538,511	$21,620,080
Percent Distribution						
Net tuition revenue	51%	51%	46%	38%	39%	38%
Auxiliary services	21%	26%	28%	33%	34%	33%
Private gifts and grants	15%	9%	10%	10%	9%	12%
Endowment and other investments	9%	10%	12%	14%	13%	13%
All other revenues	4%	4%	4%	5%	5%	4%
Full instructional expenses	$20,361,624	$20,565,240	$18,508,716	$18,508,716	$19,434,152	$20,600,201
Tuition as a percentage of full instructional expenses	82%	78%	86%	63%	65%	65%
Net tuition as a percentage of full instructional expenses	51%	45%	45%	35%	39%	40%
Operational surplus (deficit)	($164,493)	($2,398,071)	($450,455)	($1,487,808)	$104,359	$1,019,879

Figure 3.1. Proportion of Tuition Sources for Guilder and Two Peers

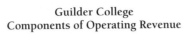

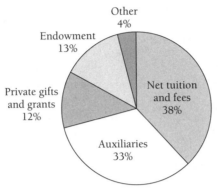

Guilder College
Components of Operating Revenue

Other 4%
Endowment 13%
Private gifts and grants 12%
Net tuition and fees 38%
Auxiliaries 33%

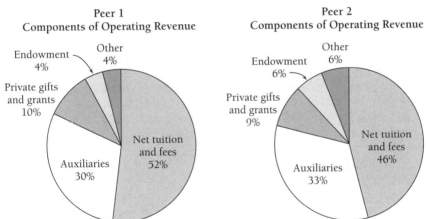

Peer 1
Components of Operating Revenue

Endowment 4%
Other 4%
Private gifts and grants 10%
Auxiliaries 30%
Net tuition and fees 52%

Peer 2
Components of Operating Revenue

Other 6%
Endowment 6%
Private gifts and grants 9%
Auxiliaries 33%
Net tuition and fees 46%

changed over time and how their tuition rates have grown. Most can then follow these statistics with a quick summary of where their tuition rates stand against their peers. These statistics have been written into the lexicon of standard management practices because the product of rate and enrollment is tuition revenue—the single largest source of revenue at most private colleges and universities and an enormously important source, if not a dominant one, in the public sector.

Still, it is useful to step back and look at tuition revenue and its twin drivers of rate and count, in the context of a formal structure of benchmarking: industry, institutional, peer, and best in class. The interplay of rate and enrollment as gross tuition revenue is perhaps best understood in the context of overall revenue sufficiency, sustainability, and balance as discussed previously.

Guilder College has struggled to manage its enrollments at its stated tuition rate. The college began the decade with a target enrollment of 280 freshmen, a level it only occasionally reached most of that time. Over the same time, Guilder experimented with tuition pricing and discounting strategies to try to buttress enrollment and earn sufficient revenues. Guilder was simultaneously trying to be careful with the messages of quality that it sent out to the market and was, therefore, self-constrained from radical shifts in enrollment strategy that might have provided revenue relief (though at a price of institutional mission and position that were unacceptable to the college).

The history of Guilder's tuition rates and enrollments is shown in Figure 3.2. Guilder experimented with holding tuition rates flat for 1992 (fiscal year 1993) and again in 1996 and 1997 (fiscal years 1997 and 1998). These periods of stability were punctuated by years of significant increases in fall 1993 and 1994 (fiscal years 1994 and 1995). Freshman enrollment (arguably the most price-sensitive group at an undergraduate institution) was volatile over these years, with a high of 280 entering in fall 1992 and a low of 228 entering in fall of 1995. Whereas certainly the discount rate and the net price paid by students was an extremely important factor in final freshman enrollment levels (and is discussed in the later section on discounting), there is an interesting indication of significant price sensitivity in Guilder's market shown in the historical relationship between the increase (decrease) in tuition rate and the (decrease) increase in enrollment. This observation was reinforced by the impact of the dramatic increase in discounting for fall 1992 in conjunction with the flat tuition rates. The demonstrated potential for significant price sensitivity among their applicant pool, in part, led to the stunning decision on the part of the college's managers and board members to decrease tuition rates for fall 1998 by nearly 30 percent (see Figure 3.2).

How did the drop in tuition rates and increase in enrollment affect revenues? Guilder would have required about sixty new freshmen to break even (in terms of gross revenues) for the freshman class. The college achieved less than that, but had hoped to bridge the differential with reduced discount rates. As discussed in detail in a following section, it did not reach that goal in the first year, though it did create what would appear to be a much sounder base from which to grow in future years. In terms of total tuition revenues, the effect of the decreased tuition rate was even more pronounced because of the small size of the preceding three entering classes. However, the financial impact of the tuition rate decrease was anticipated by the college as was the significance of the numbers.

Guilder carefully monitors its tuition rates vis-à-vis the higher education industry and the college's peer group. As of fall 2000, more than 70 percent of the undergraduates attending four-year, private colleges and universities were at institutions with stated tuition rates of $12,000 or higher. At slightly over $14,000, Guilder felt confident that its pricing is well placed against the industry range and the industry average of $16,332. By contrast, had the college continued to increase in price, even at moderate rates, from

Figure 3.2. Tuition Rates and Freshman Enrollment at Guilder

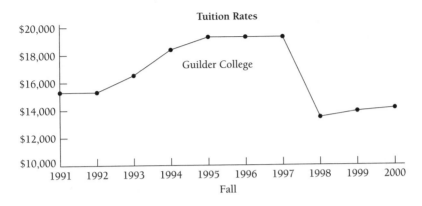

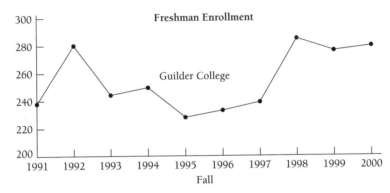

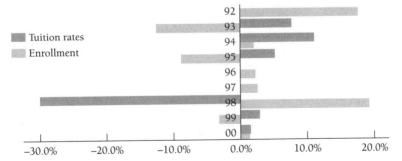

Figure 3.3. Guilder's Tuition Rates Compared with Two Peers

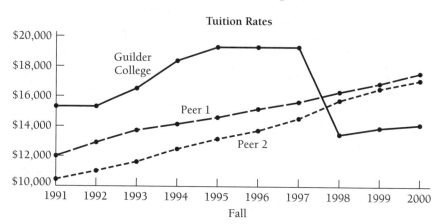

the high point of over $19,000, the college would be competing in the smallest sector (25.7 percent of undergraduates attending four-year, private colleges and universities) of the higher education market (The College Entrance Examination Board, 2001).

As compared with its peers, Guilder's rates are now lower and growing more slowly (see Figure 3.3). Guilder's tuition rate of $14,135 compares favorably with Peer 1's rate of $17,550 and Peer 2's rate of $17,100. Furthermore, its increase of 1.5 percent was well below the 4.2 percent and 3.4 percent at the peer institutions and the national average of 5.2 percent (The College Entrance Examination Board, 2001).

Guilder has identified Peer 1 as particularly successful in managing its tuition, discounting, and enrollment strategies. This comes out in consideration of all Peer 1 elements: the stability of the rate increases, stable enrollments for the first half of the decade, and predictable increases in enrollment for the second half. Guilder will continue to monitor Peer 1's progress in pricing and a variety of other attributes to see what it can learn and replicate.

Benchmarking provides insight into the drivers underlying tuition revenues. Here institutional benchmarking was particularly instructive in demonstrating the price sensitivity of Guilder's market. Peer and industry analyses of recent tuition increases suggest that Guilder might have room to increase its tuition rates a bit more quickly, once it has gained greater confidence in its ability to attract and retain the student body it desires.

Net Tuition Revenue

There are almost no institutions in the United States where gross and net tuition revenue are equal. Almost every institution discounts the tuition of some of its students. Gross tuition revenues represent only the maximum student revenue that an institution could attain; it assumes that all who attend pay fully at the stated rates. It is the net tuition revenue that defines the real institutional resources levels available to support the delivery of educational services. For tuition-dependent schools it is the critical barometer of financial resource, and for well-endowed schools an indicator of a key revenue source. Using benchmarks to understand and support the management of net tuition revenues can thus be instrumental in managing an institution's financial health.

Net tuition revenue is calculated as follows:

Gross tuition revenue – Institutional aid from all sources = Net tuition revenue

Net tuition revenue per student is calculated by dividing net tuition revenue by the count of full-time equivalent (FTE) students. The discount rate is calculated by dividing institutional aid from all sources by gross tuition revenue. The rate of tuition retention is the net tuition revenue divided by the gross tuition revenue—or, 1 minus the discount rate.

The institutional aid used in these equations is comprehensively defined. It includes *grant* aid funded by tuition dollars, other unrestricted sources, restricted funds, and endowment or foundation income. It includes financial aid used to assist students with tuition payments and financial aid used to assist students in payments for other aspects of the cost of attendance such as room and board expenses. Institutional aid, for purposes of this calculation, includes moneys awarded on a need basis and moneys awarded on a basis other than need. In short, the definition of institutional aid is comprehensive.

Net tuition revenue reflects the interplay of three factors: tuition rates, enrollment, and financial aid. It can grow with an increase in tuition rates or enrollment, or by a decrease in institutional grant aid. Changes in net tuition revenue can be looked at as the interaction of volume variance (changes in FTE students) versus price variance (changes in net tuition revenue per FTE student).

Much of the analysis of net tuition revenue has been done with first-year students, as the aid given to first-year students and the net tuition revenue that results is often a leading indicator of trends at a college or university. Upper-class aid more often reflects a continuation of the policies under which the student was accepted instead of the application of current aid policy and the institution's current ability to attract students and those students' ability and willingness to pay. Thus it may take four years of tuition, enrollment, and financial aid policies before the aggregate institutional statistics reflect their financial impact, as opposed to the more contemporaneous information that may be gained from examining the entering class.

Finally, much of the analysis of net tuition revenue has been done with full-time, undergraduate students matriculated in traditional degree programs. This is both because the bulk of financial aid is commonly directed toward these students and, frankly, because the analysis is more straightforward.

Individual institutions need to analyze their own revenue streams to find out if these are the critical drivers for their campuses. If they are, comparative data is readily available. If not, institution-specific and peer analyses may provide greater insight than trying to force the institution into these industry frameworks.

Table 3.3 shows some basic statistics on Guilder College that were used to benchmark net tuition revenue. These data points were then used to generate the statistics defined in Table 3.4. The trends show all too clearly the resource troubles that Guilder has had. Net tuition revenue in 2000–01 is roughly equal to the level in 1997–98 which in turn is lower than the high of 1995–96 and somewhere between the 1993–94 and 1994–95 levels. Drops in net tuition revenues clearly are tied to enrollment declines in years of rapidly increasing tuition rates, increasing financial aid even when tuition rates were held flat, and the inelasticity of aid necessary to attract students even in the face of a substantial tuition rate decrease. In addition, in order to keep the budget in balance or close to balance, instructional expenses (see Table 3.2) dropped by more than $2 million between 1995–96 and 1996–97. This adjustment was made a year after the significant decline in net revenues. Instructional expenses in 1999–00 are just returning to the level they were five years earlier. This clearly indicates that Guilder used significantly more of its resources during the latter half of the 1990s to attract a class through its net revenue policies than through increasing program expenditures.

National statistics place these results in a grimmer context: with little exception, Guilder has experienced greater difficulty in real net revenue generation than have comparably priced and sized higher-tuition rate, private, four-year colleges, and in the past three years has stabilized at the revenue generating capacity of lower-priced institutions. Guilder College is particularly interesting in that it bridges two categories: small colleges with higher tuition rates (SCHT) and small colleges with lower tuition rates (SCLT). Figure 3.4 compares Guilder's gross and net tuition rates with averages from these two cohorts.

Guilder then repeated this analysis with its peer schools, discovering that its net tuition revenue generation had suffered more than some and less than others. From this analysis, Guilder then selected two schools that appeared to have really gained ground in recent years. Their results and Guilder's are shown in Figure 3.5.

Guilder identified Peer 1 as being the best in class for its peer group. Peer 1, with some bumps along the way, increased enrollment, managed net tuition revenue, and increased overall net tuition resources. Peer 2 also had a strong revenue improvement over the past three years. This analysis suggested that a closer look at these two institutions could give Guilder's administrators some insight into ways to increase revenues.

Table 3.3. Basic Statistics Guilder Used to Benchmark Tuition Revenue

	1991	1992	1993	1994	1995	1996	1997	1998	1999	2000
Tuition rate	$15,356	$15,356	$16,533	$18,359	$19,294	$19,294	$19,294	$13,530	$13,926	$14,135
Full-time freshmen	238	280	245	250	228	233	239	285	276	280
Gross tuition revenue	$3,654,728	$4,299,680	$4,050,585	$4,589,750	$4,399,032	$4,495,502	$4,611,266	$3,856,050	$3,843,576	$3,957,800
Finacial aid to full-time freshmen	$1,666,103	$2,319,024	$1,872,420	$2,167,320	$1,758,852	$1,970,192	$2,270,816	$1,794,869	$1,623,455	$1,620,826

Table 3.4. Revenue Statistics for Guilder

	1991	1992	1993	1994	1995	1996	1997	1998	1999	2000
Net tuition revenue	$1,988,625	$1,980,656	$2,178,165	$2,422,430	$2,640,180	$2,525,310	$2,340,450	$2,061,181	$2,220,121	$2,336,974
Net tuition revenue per student	$8,356	$7,074	$8,890	$9,690	$11,580	$10,838	$9,793	$7,232	$8,044	$8,346
Discount rate	45.6%	53.9%	46.2%	47.2%	40.0%	43.8%	49.2%	46.5%	42.2%	41.0%
Tuition retention rate	54.4%	46.1%	53.8%	52.8%	60.0%	56.2%	50.8%	53.5%	57.8%	59.0%
Percent increases										
in tuition rate		0.0%	7.7%	11.0%	5.1%	0.0%	0.0%	−29.9%	2.9%	1.5%
in enrollment		17.6%	−12.5%	2.0%	−8.8%	2.2%	2.6%	19.2%	−3.2%	1.4%
in net tuition per student		−15.3%	25.7%	9.0%	19.5%	−6.4%	−9.6%	−26.2%	11.2%	3.8%
in net tuition revenue		−0.4%	10.0%	11.2%	9.0%	−4.4%	−7.3%	−11.9%	7.7%	5.3%

Figure 3.4. Guilder's Gross and Net Tuition Rates

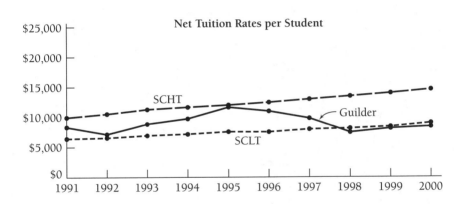

Finally, Guilder reviewed key program statistics for itself and its peers. It found that it was operating with a higher student-faculty ratio than most of the high-tuition small colleges and with fewer amenities than these schools had. Thus, its repositioning itself among the lower-priced small colleges was much more consistent with the way it was operating programmatically and thus increased its competitiveness. It had been operating among peers that it did not resemble in a variety of variables.

Discount Rates and Discount Strategies

In general, the lower the discount rate, the better. That is, if an institution's market position is strong and its price is right in that market, it can discount less and still meet enrollment and revenue targets. Assured of its financial

Figure 3.5. Impact of Enrollment, Tuition, and Aid

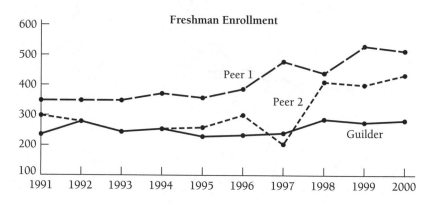

Freshman Enrollment

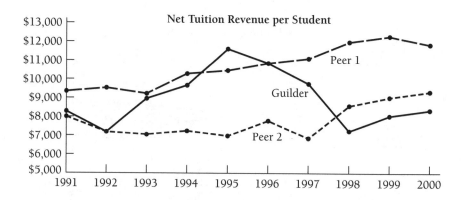

Net Tuition Revenue per Student

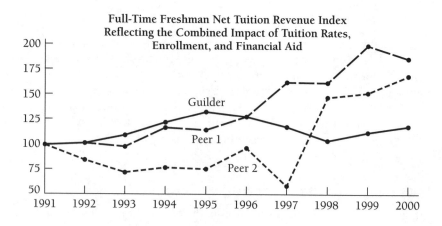

Full-Time Freshman Net Tuition Revenue Index Reflecting the Combined Impact of Tuition Rates, Enrollment, and Financial Aid

Table 3.5. Guilder's Discounting from 1991 to 2000

Fall	1991	1992	1993	1994	1995	1996[a]	1997[a]	1998[b]	1999	2000
Full-time freshmen	238	280	245	250	228	233	239	285	276	280
Discount rate		45.6%	53.9%	46.2%	47.2%	40%	43.8%	49.2%	46.5%	42.2%	41%

[a]Tuition rate held constant.
[b]Tuition rate decreased by 30 percent.

footing, an institution can focus more on the qualitative aspects of strategic discounting, such as academic quality, diversity, and gender balance.

The discount rate in and of itself means little. A low discount rate and an enrollment 25 percent below target will produce net revenue that will not meet budget. The discount rate as an absolute measure, therefore, is relevant only when enrollments are stable and the institution is at enrollment capacity. However, because enrollments are rarely stable in both quality and quantity and because capacity is a very soft concept with a number of ranges and step functions in its determination, discounting rates might be better thought of as a relative measurement or one of a group of measurements that effectively frames the question of revenue sufficiency and sustainability. Again, there is a complex relationship between institutional marketing, position in that market, the price charged, the discount offered, and the enrollment. All of these factors contribute to the college's or university's position in comparison with its own prior year data and compared with comparable institutions and industry standards.

As we have seen, Guilder College struggled with its ability to attract students at its stated tuition price. To understand its options for discounting toward a strong net tuition revenue stream, Guilder first examined its own discounting history through internal, or institutional, benchmarking (see Table 3.5).

The relationship between discounting and first-year enrollment trends is clear. In the fall of 1992 (fiscal year 1993), Guilder increased its discount substantially and saw a 17.6 percent increase in its enrollment. However, as Table 3.4 indicates, this strategy produced a slight decline of 0.04 percent in net tuition revenue due to the heavy discount. As is typical of many institutions experimenting with discounting strategies, the pendulum swung the other way for Guilder in the following year, reducing its discount rate for the class entering in the fall of 1993 and seeing a concomitant reduction in enrollment. But Table 3.4 does indicate an increase of 10 percent in net tuition revenue in fall 1992, or 2.3 percentage points better than the increase of 7.7 percent in the tuition rate. In this regard, however minimal, the strategy worked.

The pendulum swung again in fall 1995 when, in an attempt to increase net revenue (actually, to avoid issuing a significant amount of institutional grant aid), Guilder recorded its lowest discount of the decade but

Table 3.6. Freshman Tuition Discounts

Fall	1991	1992	1993	1994	1995	1996	1997	1998	1999	2000
SCHT*	31.5%	34.7%	34.6%	35.6%	37.2%	38.1%	38.0%			
SCLT*								40.6%	41.1%	41%
Guilder	45.6%	53.9%	46.2%	47.2%	40%	43.8%	49.2%	46.5%	42.2%	41%

*Source: National Association of College and University Business Officers, 2001.

also its lowest enrollment, at 228 freshmen. Referring back to Table 3.4, this time the strategy also worked, albeit in an insignificant way. Whereas enrollment declined almost 9 percent from the previous year, net tuition revenue increased 9 percent—almost 4 percentage points higher than the 5.1 percent increase in the tuition rate.

As Guilder struggled to move its first-year enrollments to fall 1992 levels, it marginally increased its discount rate in 1996 and 1997, while holding tuition flat. Enrollments were not influenced significantly; hence net revenue declined. This strategy clearly failed. In a desperate move, Guilder reduced its tuition rate in 1998 by almost 30 percent and kept its discount rate high with serious consequences to net revenue. But it was successful in increasing its enrollment, and this provided a good base for future discounting strategies. Three successive years of meeting enrollment targets and increasing net tuition revenue above rate increases seem to indicate that Guilder is on its way to using a combination of stated price and discounting strategies to its benefit.

What Guilder experienced with discounting and pricing strategies in the 1990s is all too familiar. Until 1998, it did not perform a market analysis and did not employ predictive modeling to influence its decisions. It also paid little attention to internal and external benchmarking to make reasonable assumptions. It shifted its strategies based on the previous year's results, and in so doing it lost ground in the middle part of the decade. Not until the last several years did it carefully assess its past and current positions in an informed attempt to influence its future.

To understand how Guilder compares with similar colleges nationally, administrators looked at aggregate data from small colleges with high tuition (fall 1991 to fall 1997) and then at the data from small colleges with low tuition after it reduced its rate (fall 1998 to fall 2000).

An examination of Table 3.6 and a study of Guilder's enrollments and net revenue demonstrate that the college is approaching the national industry standard tuition discount for the first time in recent history. Had it employed benchmarking, modeling, and market analysis earlier, however, it perhaps could have avoided leaving significant money on the table for much of the 1990s.

Baum (2001) cites evidence that price is a significant factor in student enrollment decisions. But she also notes that the elasticity of demand varies among different groups of students and certainly among different colleges. Low-income students have a more elastic demand than high-income students. Colleges that are in the first tier of the national rankings tend to experience a lower elasticity of demand than do colleges perceived to be less prestigious. In the latter case, price discrimination based on strategic discounting tends to impact enrollments and net revenue more than it does in the former. That is why peer group benchmarking is so vital to understanding a particular institution's experiences in the context of similarly placed schools.

Typically, peer group benchmarking should be conducted with at least ten colleges representing a range of similar institutions. There are several reasons that we recommend using that number of colleges. (1) Data are not always available from all colleges every year. (2) Some data that are confidential will be provided to you from large databases only if there are at least ten institutions in your peer group in order to preserve anonymity. (3) Most important, you do not want an institution that makes a significant change in policy to skew the peer analysis too much. For simplicity's sake, we have elected as an illustration to benchmark only two peers, one of which is also the best-in-class comparison (see Table 3.7). It is indeed important for institutions to identify an aspirant competitor among those peers to be benchmarked, in order to understand what is possible to accomplish in the context of internal and external environmental conditions.

Although these institutions are indeed peers, it is apparent that Peer 1 successfully employed a low tuition and low aid strategy to its advantage throughout the 1990s. That strategy enabled it to increase the tuition rate steadily throughout the decade with only a modest growth in the discount rate. Having performed a market analysis in 1995, and with a steadily growing applicant pool from which to draw, it built another residence hall to accommodate a planned enrollment growth starting in fall 1997. Peer 1 had determined that it had excess capacity in its academic facilities, a low enough faculty-to-student ratio, and a strong regional market to attempt this increase in enrollment without impacting institutional mission or quality. Its experience demonstrates the benefits of an integrated approach to enrollment management that uses self-promotion, internal and external benchmarking, market analysis, and tuition pricing and discounting to the institution's strategic advantage.

Guilder learned some lessons in comprehensive enrollment management from Peer 1 as it examined its peer's experiences late in the decade. It is beginning to understanding the complex mix employed by Peer 1, even though its tuition rate is now considerably lower. This presents another problem of sorts—what analysts have called the Chivas Regal Effect. If one's price is considerably lower than one's peers', students may become suspect of quality and not enroll. Guilder will have to monitor this closely in the upcoming years.

As it looks to Peer 2, Guilder can identify a pattern. Whereas lower tuition and a lower discount can produce somewhat higher enrollments if

Table 3.7. Freshman Discount Rates and Enrollment: Guilder versus Peers

Fall	1991	1992	1993	1994	1995	1996[a]	1997[a]	1998[b]	1999	2000
Guilder										
Full-time freshmen	238	280	245	250	228	233	239	285	276	280
Discount rate	45.6%	53.9%	46.2%	47.2%	40%	43.8%	49.2%	46.5%	42.2%	41%
Tuition rate	$15,356	$15,356	$16,533	$18,359	$19,294	$19,294	$19,294	$13,530	$13,926	$14,135
Peer 1 (best in class)										
Full-time freshmen	350	350	349	375	358	388	479	440	532	514
Discount rate	21.9%	26.6%	33.2%	27.6%	28.8%	28.8%	29.2%	26.5%	27.3%	32.6%
Tuition rate	$11,970	$13,000	$13,800	$14,200	$14,650	$15,190	$15,650	$16,300	$16,850	$17,550
Peer 2										
Full-time freshmen	295	281	244	256	258	298	204	411	401	434
Discount rate	22.7%	35.2%	39.7%	42.6%	47.8%	43.6%	53.3%	45.6%	45.3%	45.6%
Tuition rate	$10,470	$11,030	$11,630	$12,530	$13,230	$13,790	$14,590	$15,790	$16,530	$17,100

[a]Guilder tuition rate held constant.

[b]Guilder tuition rate decreased by 30 percent.

combined with informed market analyses, Peer 2 lost ground to Guilder throughout the decade. As shown in Figure 3.4, Guilder's net tuition revenue per student exceeded Peer 2's experiences until Guilder decided to lower its tuition in 1998. At the same time, Peer 2 experienced a dramatic decrease in freshmen enrollment in 1997 due less to its discounting strategies and more to the departure of the dean of admissions in August and its inability to replace that position in a timely fashion. Peer 2 has since moved to a comprehensive enrollment management model and, like Peer 1, has set about increasing its enrollment significantly. Unlike Peer 1, however (and not apparent from this benchmarking data), Peer 2 increased its enrollment by sacrificing student quality, something Guilder has been unwilling to do.

This brings us to our final point in benchmarking discount rates and determining discounting strategies. Industry, internal, best-in-class, and peer benchmarking can help an institution understand its relative position in key performance indicators, and it can clarify major areas for improvement. But the goals of maximizing enrollments to capacity and increasing net tuition revenue to operate the institution must be related to the college's mission and values. Discounting strategies can be targeted to increase certain groups of students—students of color, first-generation college students, and full payers who otherwise would not enroll without some level of discount.

Putting It All Together

A critical factor for an institution considering pricing policies that have the potential of increasing or decreasing the institution's enrollment is what impact these policies will have on the operating costs of the college. First, it is incumbent on an institution to determine its optimum size. An institution should assess how many students it can physically accommodate and how many students its faculty and academic programs are designed to handle. It is then reasonable to look at the size of its peer institutions. An institution often wants to have an enrollment of a similar size to its peers as students often look at similarly sized colleges. Its enrollment management strategy should be guided in part by the total enrollment that the institution wants to achieve.

The costs that an institution must look at are the instruction and instruction-related costs—the full instructional expenses in Table 3.2. Average cost analysis across the entire student body will not, however, be very useful in making decisions about the appropriate tuition discounting strategies. Institutions should analyze the impact an additional one, ten, or a hundred students will have on the costs of the institution. How much more will an institution have to spend if one more student enrolls?

We are really asking the question of how the institution's costs relate to its capacity. How many students can the institution's facilities accommodate? Is there excess classroom space? Library space? Space in the student center? The residence halls? If the answer to all of these questions is yes, clearly the facilities can accommodate more students without any increase in facility costs. Additional questions may center on the changes that will occur in student life with more students. Will they be positive or negative? These questions clearly extend beyond the dollars and cents but are critical to making wise decisions as a decrease in the quality of life at an institution will make it harder to recruit and enroll students.

Alternatively, if the institution's facilities are at capacity, additional students will require major new capital investment. Thus, additional students will cost the institution far more than the average cost of the existing students. Benchmarking frequently is used to analyze facility capacity. Institutions can benchmark with themselves and changes over time, with peer institutions to ensure that they provide similar space per student, and with the best in class to see what they may want to aspire to.

The next set of questions to investigate is the relationship between faculty and students. What is the current student faculty ratio at the institution? Is it above or below the institution's desired level? How does it compare with the college's historical level? How does it compare with peer institutions and to best in class? If it is lower than optimal, more students can be enrolled without the need for additional faculty, although differences between certain majors and upper and lower division courses often are masked in this type of analysis. Strategies that provide an enrollment equilibrium often require treating different groups of students quite differently in terms of discounting strategies. Some institutions are uncomfortable with the equity issues these differential strategies raise.

Strategies to achieve institutional enrollment goals are numerous and complex. A great deal of time has been spent on how institutions can provide students with discounts to achieve their enrollment goals. For institutions that are under-enrolled, colleges often discount from the published price to increase the enrollment. For institutions that are operating with the level of enrollment that they want, discounts often are used to shape the class for quality or net revenue gains.

Guilder's situation called for a drastic solution. Its benchmarking analysis indicated that it was not operating in many ways like institutions that charged high tuition. Guilder needed to reposition itself and move into a different national peer group—it moved from small schools with high tuition to small schools with low tuition. It is important to look at the industry and to compare an institution with others on a variety of measures and with different benchmarks.

Up to a point, discounting may indeed increase revenue. Beyond that, the extent of discounting is a decision that institutions make to forgo revenue to shape the student body in a variety of ways versus collecting those funds and spending them directly on programmatic enhancements. Will an institution get a stronger student body by providing scholarships to student leaders or high school valedictorians or by increasing the number of full-time faculty or providing some unique academic programs? Benchmarking helps influence these decisions. For example, some institutions are providing free computers to all of its students; is this more effective in attracting students than a scholarship? Do the computers accomplish multiple goals in terms of academic programming as well as increasing the attractiveness of the institution? These are all very complex and difficult issues.

Colleges and universities continually must make complex trade-offs, balancing their role, mission, and values with financial viability. Ambitious goals are admirable, but when they lead to a deficit on the bottom line they require a change of course. Benchmarking against an institution's past, against a national database, against a select group of peer institutions, and against best in class can provide a clear and informed framework for institutional decisions.

References

Alstete, J. W. *Benchmarking in Higher Education: Adapting Best Practices to Improve Quality.* ASHE-ERIC Higher Education Report, no. 5. San Francisco: Jossey-Bass, 1995.

Baum, S. *Higher Education: Dollars and Sense.* New York: College Entrance Examination Board, 2001.

College Entrance Examination Board. *Trends in College Pricing.* Washington, D.C.: College Entrance Examination Board, 2001.

Halstead, K. *Tuition Fact Book 1998, A Compendium of Data Analysis.* Arlington, Va.: Research Associates of Washington, 1998.

Lapovsky, L., and Loomis Hubbell, L. W. "An Uncertain Future." *Business Officer,* Feb. 2001, pp. 24–31.

National Association of College and University Business Officers. *2000 Tuition Discounting Survey.* Washington, D.C.: National Association of College and University Business Officers, 2001.

LOREN W. LOOMIS HUBBELL *is vice president for administration and finance, Hobart and William Smith Colleges.*

ROBERT J. MASSA *is vice president of enrollment, student life, and college relations, Dickinson College.*

LUCIE LAPOVSKY *is president, Mercy College.*

4

Joining the Big Ten wasn't just about football. Since it became part of the alliance, Penn State has learned to benchmark to great effect, particularly in regard to faculty and academic issues.

Penn State Joins the Big Ten and Learns to Benchmark

Robert Secor

In December 1989, when I was one of the officers of Penn State's faculty senate, President Bryce Jordan asked to meet with us in advance of a major announcement. Penn State had agreed to join the Big Ten consortium. While visions of Rose Bowls danced in our heads, President Jordan, to our surprise, said that the major significance of the move for us was in academics. Joining the alliance would allow us to form academic relationships with the group of institutions most similar to us: Illinois, Indiana, Iowa, Michigan, Michigan State, Minnesota, Northwestern, Ohio State, Purdue, and Wisconsin. All but Northwestern is a public university, all are Association of American Universities (AAU) research universities, and seven are land grant institutions. Moreover, they all have strong academic reputations and always are listed among the top third public universities in the country, several usually listed among the best half-dozen such schools.

Jordan suggested that, in terms of overall academic excellence, we probably placed somewhere in the middle of this group. As a result, we would have a comparative group from which we could learn, particularly in regard to those schools that were doing better than us in certain areas. Jordan was talking benchmarking without even knowing it. Allan Bolton establishes as a first principle of benchmarking finding a "family of like institutions" (Bolton, 2000, p. 129), whereas Middaugh (2001) recounts the elaborate efforts undertaken to establish such a peer group in the Delaware Study (pp. 91–123). Our president had just found us one by joining a football conference.

65

Benchmarking for Strategic Purposes

When the following year I was asked to head the English department, the comparative base the Big Ten offered me could not have been more timely. As I looked over the past correspondence from previous department heads to our deans, I noticed a growing trend–and a growing exasperation—as the heads commented on the increasing shrinkage of the tenured faculty and the concurrent increased reliance on fixed-term (or adjunct) faculty. Strategic plans from our department had no impact when we asserted that we needed to raise our faculty numbers from our current fifty-six to the seventy that we had at our height. What we needed, I was convinced, was a way of showing that our figures were out of line with comparative institutions, and then to understand what these institutions were doing differently. In other words, although I didn't know the terms yet, we had to do both competitive and process benchmarking.

Our dean also urged us to develop performance indicators, measures to show her that we were worth investing in. We developed a list of ten journals that we thought had the strongest reputation in the discipline, then spent weeks of library research looking for institutional identifications of Committee on Institutional Cooperation (CIC) schools for the authors of all articles and notes published in them from 1981 through 1985. (The CIC consists of all of the schools in the Big Ten and the University of Chicago, which had been in the Big Ten before it withdrew from its athletic competition, but then joined the CIC when it was formed in 1958.) Then we did the same for the years 1986 to 1990. The data we created showed marked improvement in the publication numbers in the more recent period, and a steady rise in our standing in relation to our peers. We then benchmarked data with the same group: numbers of standing faculty, numbers of graduate students, numbers of teaching assistants, TA stipends, teaching loads for faculty and TAs, and undergraduate majors (see Table 4.1).

What we could show was that among the public institutions, only three of our Big Ten peers had fewer professorial faculty than we did, but we had more than twice as many lecturers and instructors than our nearest competitor. Whereas we had seventy-five such members in our department, only Purdue, Ohio State, Michigan, and Minnesota also were in double figures. We knew we had unique problems, but we did not know the degree of difference until we had these figures. We also learned that our 140 graduate students were the lowest in our comparative group (Indiana and Minnesota had 300), and our TA numbers were more than twenty-five under the average for the other public institutions. With our teaching assistants teaching four courses a year for us at the time, an additional twenty-five would add one hundred sections a year, allowing for a major reduction in our fixed-term faculty.

The only numbers on our benchmarking chart that did not serve our interests were those for undergraduate majors, where we placed close to the

Table 4.1. Comparative Data for English Departments at Big Ten Universities—1991

	Illinois	Indiana	Iowa	Michigan State	Michigan	Minnesota	Northwestern	Ohio State	Penn State	Purdue	Wisconsin
Faculty											
Standing professors	25	30	33	36	32	26	8	24	19	20.7	31
Associates	25	20	6	15	23	11.5	8	25	26	17.8	14
Assistants	15	13	9	9	14	5.5	8	23	13	11.5	10
Total	65	63	48	60	69	43	24	72	58	50	55
Lecturers and instructors	4	6	4	2	33.9	10	9	20	75	17	na
Graduate students (in residence)											
M.A.	0	100	15	143	84	100	90	160	52	97	50
M.F.A.	0	50	110	0	0	0	0	0	31	0	0
Ph.D.	150	150	105	117	120	200	50	60	57	133	100
Total	150	300	230	260	204	300	140	220	140	230	150
Teaching assistants	150	140	83	73	144	40	50	145	80	92.3	100
TA stipends	$2,500 per section	$2,546–$2,774 per section	na	na	$3336–4710 per section	$2440 per section	na	$7839–8793 per year	$7780–9320 per year	na	$11,000 per year
Teaching load (per academic year)											
Standing faculty	4	4	4	6	4	5	5	5	4	na	4
Graduate students	3	3	3	3	3	3	3	3	3	2	2
Undergraduate majors	775	887	825	765	923	450	380	821	550	591	na

bottom. We did worry that they would undermine our argument for the need for more faculty lines, but we decided to include them for the sake of credibility. We could always make the point that most of our teaching was in service areas and for non-majors. We might even try to make the case that our low faculty numbers had a negative impact on the majors we could draw, so that if anything, the numbers argued in favor of increasing our faculty strength. It is amazing how fast we learned the strategies of benchmarking.

Of course, we did not make our case simply with benchmarking figures. We offered to make sacrifices to contribute to the costs of funding our requests—from agreeing among ourselves to variable teaching loads to increase our productivity, to eliminating weak and costly programs, such as our nonfiction writing program and our minor in technical writing. As a result of the new and stronger faculty we have been able to recruit over the past decade with our new openings, and with strong departmental leadership after I left, the department has risen in the rankings from forty-one to twenty-seven. Alan Bolton talks about the positive possibilities for strategic planning when benchmarking is properly used: "The benefits are likely to be considerable—and may make a new, direct and powerful contribution to your strategic planning and development and to making more persuasive the business plans which you place before institutional bodies and external bodies" (2000, p. 130). The Department of English at Penn State does not have to be convinced.

Benchmarking Tenure and Promotion Procedures

Several years later, a different president, Joab Thomas, and the chair of the faculty senate asked me to chair a committee to review our tenure and promotion policies. It took a number of phone calls to our Big Ten colleagues to set up a database that would serve as a context for our own discussions (see Table 4.2).

Among the information we sought was the frequency of their provisional reviews, the levels of review (we were surprised how few used a university-level committee, as we do), the degree to which they linked tenure and promotion, and the effective date of tenure. We found places where the Penn State system is very different from most of our colleagues, as in our series of formal second-, third-, and fourth-year reviews, but where we decided that our system serves us best. Other findings, however, led us to make changes, as in our effective date of tenure, from the end to the beginning of the seventh year. Like our peers we now presume that promotion and tenure at the sixth year will be linked. Since moving to the provost's office in 1995, with responsibility for the promotion and tenure process, I have continued to make use of this study and to share best practices with my counterparts in the Big Ten.

The Committee on Institutional Cooperation

Seven years after Jordan called us into his office to announce our entry into the Big Ten, Provost John Brighton commented to our board of trustees: "It is my belief that the decision to join the Big Ten, and the implementation of that decision, was the greatest accomplishment of Bryce Jordan's presidency and the most important move made by the university in the last quarter of a century" (Jan. 19, 1996). As it was for Jordan, however, for Brighton the basis for his belief was not the impact on our athletic program, but rather our entry into the Big Ten's academic consortium, the CIC. None of the other football conferences have a similar academic counterpart. As Brighton concluded, "In athletics we improve through competition with strong opponents. In academics we improve through comparing with outstanding institutions and collaborating with quality colleagues."

CIC Collaborating and Benchmarking Groups. Working with a CIC director, staff, and office based at Urbana-Champaign, CIC institutions recognize their collective strength, share resources, collaborate, and benchmark. The CIC board consists of all of the CIC provosts, who generally meet three times a year at Chicago's O'Hare Airport, but they communicate with each other throughout the year. In addition to our provosts, there are more than one hundred groups or subgroups of people from our twelve institutions who similarly meet to share data and best practices on a continual basis. As one of those groups, English department chairs benchmark data and compare stories and concerns, and I always came away from those meetings with some ideas to try out on our colleagues.

Perhaps the most active group within the CIC is our librarians. Under the CIC Center for Library Initiatives, the librarians have not only benchmarked most areas, but they have developed significant shared resources and programs that have greatly expanded the opportunities for faculty productivity. The CIC has also been a strong meeting ground for research, and a CIC World Wide Web site identifies the senior research officers as a group that carries on an "active consortial program of information exchange and policy discussion and action," with "active subgroups that include the Research Integrity Officers and the Technology Transfer Officers, to share ideas and best practices and to pursue common agendas within the CIC" (Committee on Institutional Cooperation, n.d.).

Benchmarking by E-Mail. Normally, CIC groups meet once or twice a year, but their greatest value comes from the connections made at these meetings and the ability to use e-mail and listservs afterward to benchmark and learn best practices. Such e-mail benchmarking can be a continuing process, and the results can impact several schools at once. For example, about five years ago I sent out a query concerning exit-interview questionnaires, because Penn State wanted to devise one for faculty departing the university. One of my fellow associate provosts sent me back a questionnaire that we found very useful, and we adapted it for the program we were

Table 4.2. Promotion and Tenure Practices at the CIC Instituitions

Institution	Frequency of Reviews	Levels of Review	Linking Promotion and Tenure	Effective Date of Tenure
Chicago	Formal review at the end of the third year; final review in the sixth year	Sixth-year review by department, department head, graduate division dean, and provost	Linked; granting of tenure comes with promotion, and promotion comes with tenure	July 1 following approval (beginning of the seventh year)
Illinois-Urbana and Champaign	Formal review no later than third year; more frequent reviews recommended	Sixth-year review at the department or school, college campus or graduate dean levels	Not formally tied, but typically promotion comes with tenure, and granting of tenure comes with promotion	Beginning of the seventh year (or the first year following approval)
Indiana-Bloomington	Annual review at the department level only	P&T reviews at the department, college, or school and campus levels	Tenure includes promotion to associate professor; promotion does not automatically bring tenure	Beginning of the eighth year
Iowa	Annual reviews, reported to deans and vice president for academic affairs	Recommendations of department committee, department head, and dean submitted to vice president for academic affairs	Tenure is tied to promotion to associate professor; promotion from assistant professor to associate professor is tied to tenure	Tenure becomes effective on the date of appointment in the following (seventh) year
Michigan-Ann Arbor	Informal review at three years; formal review at six years	Divisional committee, department chair, college executive committee, provost, regents	Promotion to associate professor or professor usually comes with tenure; granting of tenure automatically brings promotion to associate professor	Beginning of the seventh year
Michigan State	Informal annual reviews	Department, sometimes college; recommendations reviewed successively by dean and provost	If assistant professor is promoted to associate professor, then tenure is granted. Tenure usually tied to promotion.	Effective upon the first day of the month after the date of approval by the board
Minnesota	Annual review by department; final tenure review by end of six year	Department, dean, college committee optional, vice president for academic affairs, university committee optional	Promotion to associate professor or professor must be with tenure. Tenure to assistant professor usually accompanied by promotion.	Beginning of the seventh year (or fall term after the final review)

Northwestern	Formal review in third year by department and dean; formal review in sixth year	Not automatic, but almost without exception, the granting of tenure to assistant professor is accompanied by promotion to associate professor	Final review by department, schoolwide committee, dean, and provost	Beginning of the seventh year (or first day of the next academic year)
Ohio State	Annual informal review (department); formal fourth year (department and college); formal sixth-year review	Rarely tenure without promotion to associate professor, and rarely promotion to associate professor without tenure	Department committee, head, college committee, dean, university committee, senior vice president or provost	Beginning of the seventh year
Purdue	Annual reviews by heads of department or schools and deans	Automatic tenure with promotion to associate professor or professor; no automatic promotion with tenure to assistant professor	Department committee, department head, area committee, dean, executive vice president of provost	Beginning of the seventh year
Wisconsin-Madison	Annual review by an oversight committee	Not formally linked, but tenure is no longer granted without promotion to associate professor, and promotions almost always come with tenure	Department committee, head, division executive committee, dean, provost, vice chancellor for academic affairs	The year following approval by the regents in June (beginning of the seventh year)

building. That program has developed into an extensive process that includes not only the questionnaire but face-to-face interviews for all departing faculty with a college exit interview officer. We hold annual meetings with our exit interview officers and discuss each year's findings with our deans and the Senate Committee on Faculty Affairs. Last year came the call on my peer group listserv asking if any of us had developed an exit interview program. The program I was able to share, which as a result is now being adapted at another CIC school, was built on the questionnaire that was first developed more than six years earlier, not by either of us, but by a third school on our party line.

Reviewing my inbox for the past several weeks, I find the following examples of e-mail benchmarking. My peers are constantly seeking best practices related to faculty issues:

> We have one official reason for extending the pre-tenure probationary period—parenting responsibilities—but as a matter of fact, extensions are given for other reasons as well (e.g., delay of lab set-up; excessive clinical duties in the medical school), and we're considering putting together a set of principles for extensions. Do you have any such policies or guidelines that cover extensions OTHER THAN due to parenting? If so, could you point me to a website where I might find them, send them to me as an attachment, or otherwise give me information about them? Thanks so much.

The following exchange on mentoring was particularly informative, particularly for us at Penn State, because this is an issue on which we too are currently focusing. Kathleen Pecknold, associate provost and director of academic human resources at the University of Illinois, wrote:

> Hello. Here at Illinois, we are reviewing current faculty mentoring programs, particularly those for women and minorities. Do any of you have formal programs at the central campus level? If so, would you send me information/URL's etc please? If not, is there any way to give me information about decentralized programs? I would appreciate any and all information. Thanks in advance!

Among the responses she received was one from Lee Anna Clark, associate provost for faculty, University of Iowa, who said in part: "Just this fall I surveyed colleges about their collegiate and departmental mentoring programs. A summary of their responses is attached." The summary describes a variety of mentoring efforts in ten colleges at the University of Illinois. The College of Business has "a formal, voluntary program for all probationary faculty in their first three-year appointment"; the College of Dentistry "runs a well-attended Junior Faculty Seminar Series," started under an NIH grant; the College of Education invites faculty in their first three years to join a New Faculty Group, which meets monthly to discuss programs suggested by the group and offered by the college; in the College of Engineering, mentoring takes place at the departmental level; the Dean of the College of Law appoints a faculty member for all new faculty; the College of Liberal Arts has an extensive set of activities for new faculty, monitors mentoring programs in the college's departments, and claims that all departments offer some sort of mentoring; the College of Medicine describes the Faculty Mentoring program that it is now launching. Clark concludes by saying: "The Provost Office hopes to compile a 'Handbook for Faculty Mentoring at the University of Iowa,' that will contain additional information about (a) the mentoring programs throughout the University that are summarized above, so that the college and departmental administrators can learn from each other's successes and (b) good mentoring practices gleaned from the literature on the topic with citations of additional resource materials that are available." Clearly the attempt at Illinois is to benchmark best practices among its various units to improve mentoring programs throughout the university, but Illinois's experiences have now become part of the larger benchmarking exercise of our CIC peer group as those of us who share responsibility for faculty personnel issues respond to Kathleen's e-mail request.

Benchmarking Academic Leadership in the CIC

The development of academic leadership programs also comes under my umbrella of responsibilities, and here too I have relied on the benchmarking opportunities afforded by our entry into the Big Ten. Five years ago, for example, I was involved in initiating an annual CIC program for department heads, chairs, and school and program directors. We call it a Department Executive Officers (DEO) program, a term borrowed from the University of Iowa. The program brings experienced and new DEOs together to talk about common concerns and successful practices in leading an academic unit at the department level.

The program is modeled in part in part on the CIC's Academic Leadership Program (ALP), now in its twelfth year, and the jewel of the consortium's leadership programs. The ALP brings academic leaders and potential leaders together at one of our campuses for a three-day seminar three times a year.

Benchmarking at the College Level

A few years ago, the university guidelines for strategic planning specifically required all colleges to identify critical processes for improvement and a benchmarking plan. Because not all of our colleges have exact counterparts at every CIC institution, and some colleges outside the consortium may have particular strengths and practices that should be considered, our colleges are encouraged to supplement or substitute the peer group to achieve

Table 4.3. Big Ten Calendar Summary

Universities on the Semester System	Fall Semester Instruction	Fall Semester Exams	Spring Semester Instruction	Spring Semester Exams	Total Instruction Days	Total Instruction Plus Exams
Illinois	72	6	72	6	144	156
Indiana	72	5	74	5	146	156
Iowa	75	5	74	5	149	159
Michigan	69	6	68	6	137	149
Michigan State*	71	5	71	5	142	152
Minnesota	72	6	74	6	146	158
Penn State	75	5	75	5	150	160
Purdue	73	6	75	6	148	160
Wisconsin	72	6	74	6	146	158

Universities on the Quarter System	First-Quarter Instruction	First-Quarter Exams	Second-Quarter Instruction	Second-Quarter Exams	Third-Quarter Instruction	Third-Quarter Exams	Total Instruction Days	Total Instruction Plus Exams
Northwestern	53	6	50	6	49	6	152	170
Ohio State	50	4	49	4	49	4	148	160

*Spring 2001 figures; Spring 2002 not available.

the most appropriate competitive benchmarking for their discipline. Our Smeal College of Business Administration, for example, has created what it calls an affinity group of institutions, consisting of sixteen schools: eight CIC institutions and eight other public doctoral and research universities. In 1995, our College of Engineering launched a major benchmarking program by sending continuous quality improvement (CQI) teams to Purdue, Illinois, Georgia Tech, Virginia Tech, and Maryland. At each institution, the team benchmarked undergraduate program assessment, graduate student recruitment, industry interface, minorities in engineering, and women in engineering. For this last topic, they had the context of the CIC Women in Science and Engineering (WISE) Initiative, which has been holding WISE best practices workshops since 1997. In addition to submitting separate reports for each school, the teams submitted a summary of benchmarking team highlights that they garnered from their review of the five campuses.

The Teaching and Learning Consortium and Internal Benchmarking

In July 1999, Penn State established its universitywide Teaching and Learning Consortium (TLC). The consortium established six teams, including a department head team, a faculty team, a student team, and a teaching assistant team. These teams were to discuss the teaching and learning processes from their various perspectives and gather and share best pedagogical practices. The teaching assistant team, for example, sent out a notice to all TA supervisors and coordinators and graduate program officers to begin sharing information. Thirty-five departments attended a workshop to discuss better preparation and development of TAs based on proven techniques and shared resources for continued growth and development.

Clearly the methodology (and terminology) reflected the principles conveyed by our CQI office, and I know of no program that has undertaken a more thorough process of internal benchmarking than has the TLC. Some of its products to date include a list of "Effective Practices for Improving Learning," a "Report for Effective Practices for Teaching Assistants," a statement of "'Best Practices' for Department Heads for Improving Teaching and Learning," a list of "Department-wide Initiatives for Improving Learning," and a Web site connecting other teaching and learning units throughout the university. These best practice documents—available on the TLC Web site—have been presented and discussed at our Academic Leadership Forum seminars for department heads. Last spring there was a TLC colloquy that focused on sharing best teaching and learning practices and featured academic departments that had received small grants to improve teaching and learning.

The Office of Human Resources

There is probably more benchmarking activity taking place in our Office of Human Resources than anyplace else in the university. The office benchmarks with the CIC and the AAU, as well as other universities and colleges in Pennsylvania; with professional societies, and at times with business and industry. It benchmarks benefits packages, insurance coverage, dual-career assistance programs, recruitment approaches, salary increases, training and development programs, adoption policies, and work and life issues, including child-care facilities—to name just a few. Many of its studies result in reports that come through the Senate Committee on Faculty Benefits; given the fact that our university has twenty-three locations within the state, these reports often involve internal as well as external benchmarking. Every other year, for example, a report is developed for presentation at the faculty senate comparing salaries for all of our colleges and our twenty-three locations inside Pennsylvania, whereas comparative salary figures are benchmarked with our CIC colleagues in alternate years.

The Faculty Senate

Benchmarking, particularly within our CIC cohort, has not only become a useful informational tool for our faculty senate, but it has also allowed us to establish contexts to achieve the ends of shared governance. Let me give a recent example.

About two years ago, the administration indicated a need to create a policy on intellectual property related to the development of Web-based courses. Like most universities, Penn State felt there needed to be some understanding concerning ownership of such courses developed by faculty, and as at most other universities, this began as a contentious issue. It was understandable that faculty members, who were used to owning the text-books they wrote and the profits they brought in, could not understand why they did not fully own the courses they developed on the Web. But it was also understandable why the university, which was becoming heavily invested in the development and delivery of Web-based courses, was not ready to allow these courses to become its competition. Helping us see our way through the thicket was the CIC consortium. The Copyright and Intellectual Property Committee of the CIC held a two-day conference in September 1999, attended by more than sixty representatives from twelve CIC members. Participants shared policies from the several schools that already had them, entered into vigorous discussions and analyses, and issued a report setting out some guidelines and common beliefs. The report set a context for Penn State's task force, and when it reported to the faculty senate it was able to state that it

> recognized the importance of interacting with other universities to learn about "best practices" of intellectual property administration issues and opportunities. Information from other universities—including Indiana, MIT, North Carolina State, Stanford University, University of Florida, University of Illinois, University of Michigan, University of North Carolina, University of Texas, and the University of Washington—was gathered from a variety of sources: web sites, telephone surveys, interviews with Penn State creators of intellectual property and start-up companies, copies of reports from institutions that have recently reviewed their policies and procedures, the CIC Conference on Copyright held on September 23–24, 1999, at the University of Illinois, attendance at intellectual property conferences, and the teleconference on copyright sponsored by the Association of Research Libraries and National Association of State Universities and Land-Grant Colleges (NASULGC). [Report to the faculty senate, April 20, 2001]

The task force "selected a number of universities for benchmarking via a phone survey. The information on their home pages was reviewed and followed by an in-depth telephone conference with designated faculty and staff. Most of the benchmark universities are also dealing with the same intellectual property-related issues as Penn State." Benchmarking thus showed that the issue was not just one of local administrative concern.

The report went on to say that "The majority of the institutions indicated that one of their primary goals was to generate revenue. Another important goal is the service provided to faculty inventors. Several institutions indicated that generating revenues, building equity, increasing sponsored research funding, and providing service to faculty inventors and society are all necessary goals of the institution." In other words, our colleagues at other institutions who had already wrestled with the issue indicated that there was faculty as well as administrative interest in achieving a policy. Benchmarking thus made the intellectual property policy understandable and acceptable to the faculty senators while it presented solutions that the administration may not have felt went far enough if it had not seen the data from the benchmarked institutions. The policy passed by a wide margin at the faculty senate last spring.

Summing Up

I have tried to show how Penn State's joining the Big Ten created for us a peer group that has allowed significant and successful benchmarking that was previously unavailable to us, and that, with the establishment of our Office for Continuous Quality Improvement almost immediately afterward, we have learned to take every advantage of that opportunity. Benchmarking occasions reach every part of the university, and beyond: our Campus Community Partnership recently sent a fact-finding mission to the University of Iowa so the university and State College Borough police officers could observe how other college towns deal with alcohol enforcement, town and gown relations, and riots. It is not surprising, though, that the greatest emphasis in our benchmarking efforts seems to relate to faculty interests and issues—teaching, benefits, salaries, tenure and promotion, research, library resources, faculty development, and building academic strength within the department. In this regard we are not so different from business and industry. In its most recent annual report, BenchNet: The Benchmarking Exchange (2001) listed the most actively benchmarked business processes from the preceding year, and employee development finished in first place. Penn State has not attended many Rose Bowls since 1990, but as Bryce Jordan foresaw, our academic and faculty issues have been greatly served by our ability to benchmark with and learn from our consortium of academic peers.

References

BenchNet: The Benchmarking Exchange. "Benchmarking—Past, Present and Future: An Annual Report." [http://www.benchnet.com/bppf2001.htm]. Jan. 2001.

Bolton, A. *Managing the Academic Unit.* Philadelphia: Open University Press, 2000

Committee on Institutional Cooperation. "Research at CIC Universities." [http://www.cic.uiuc.edu/resources/institutions/SRO.html]. n.d.

Middaugh, M. *Understanding Faculty Productivity.* San Francisco: Jossey-Bass, 2001.

ROBERT SECOR *is provost and professor at Pennsylvania State University.*

5

*This chapter explores benchmarks of quality for distance
education and considers the unique perspectives of the
various stakeholders promoting these benchmarks.*

Benchmarking Distance Education

Richard J. Novak

Distance education is one of the most controversial topics in higher education today. Whereas distance learning has a long history, dating back to nineteenth-century correspondence courses, modern technologies have transformed the landscape for courses that are not campus-based. College and university administrators, faculty, and students, as well as accrediting bodies, have debated the challenges that distance learning presents to the academy, and many fear the demise of the academy in its current form. The need for expanding opportunities and access to higher education is generally a point of agreement, but the manner in which those opportunities are offered and supervised has become a major focus of debate.

Specifically, the debate has centered on academic quality. How can we measure the quality of student learning if we do not know who is at the other end of an Internet connection? Is the quality of student learning equal to that offered in traditional modes? And, most critical, is the quality of the degree earned by a student through distance learning the same as that of the student who earned the degree in a standard classroom setting? This chapter will identify and discuss the myriad perspectives pertaining to measures of quality and benchmarking in distance education. It will also review the standards or benchmarks of quality that have been promulgated by various stakeholder groups.

Perspectives

The common theme that emerges in questions about quality in distance learning is the following: How do we know what constitutes quality in distance learning, since we do not have benchmarks on which to base our

NEW DIRECTIONS FOR HIGHER EDUCATION, no. 118, Summer 2002   © Wiley Periodicals, Inc.

decisions? The expansion of distance learning opportunities has come so fast that measures of quality for such factors as course offerings, pricing, learning outcomes, and academic support are not long-standing normative values. Faculty across the country make passionate statements regarding the need for academic freedom in distance learning while decrying the anticipated decline of educational quality. Local governments and businesses stress that new learning methodologies must be geared to meet the needs of the workforce. At the same time, educational researchers readily dismiss comparisons between e-learning and traditional classroom instruction, saying that they do not yield important differences or fruitful findings (Verduin and Clark, 1991; Russell, 1999). While the two methods may be different, often there is no significant difference between them in terms of learning outcomes. Other academicians call for a better understanding and emphasis on adult learning (Gibson, 1998), and accrediting agencies struggle with the application of traditional measures to meet new learning styles. To paraphrase a proverb, While beauty may be in the eye of the beholder, quality benchmarks appear to be in the eye of the stakeholder. In other words, whereas there is some consensus about what constitutes quality in distance education, there is also significant divergence that is directly related to the specific interests of the various stakeholders.

Academic leaders who are concerned about the quality of distance education programs and the development of benchmarks to identify and measure quality face an enormous task. They first need to become familiar with the numerous statements about quality and benchmark standards that have been promulgated by professional associations and accrediting agencies. Included in this process is, of course, a critical analysis of these statements, with attention to any special interests of the stakeholder group that may influence the benchmarks. Leaders also must become thoroughly familiar with the research of distance learning while taking into account consensus points from the various perspectives and their own personal history and educational experiences. The final step is to acknowledge that distance learning is an evolving medium and that what we are calling distance education today will probably be unrecognizable ten years from now.

The IHEP Report

The Institute for Higher Education Policy (IHEP), a nonprofit, nonpartisan organization, in April 2000 published "Quality on the Line: Benchmarks for Success in Internet-based Distance Education" (Institute for Higher Education Policy, 2000). This publication is one of the most comprehensive statements regarding quality in distance education. Interestingly, it was prepared with support from the National Education Association, the largest professional association of higher education faculty, and Blackboard, one of the top three business providers of a software platform for delivering online courses.

The IHEP report identifies multiple benchmarks for use in distance learning; it was developed through a three-step process to help ensure the inclusiveness and accuracy of its recommendations. The first phase included a comprehensive literature search of benchmarks recommended by policy groups, educational organizations, and several leading experts in higher education; the search yielded forty-five benchmarks. The second phase involved identifying institutions that "have substantial experience and are providing leadership in distance education" (p. 9). The third phase involved surveying each of the identified institutions and visits by IHEP staff to assess the degree to which these institutions incorporated the benchmarks. A total of 147 respondents representing six participating institutions were interviewed or surveyed. As a result, the list of forty-five benchmarks was reduced to twenty-four, organized in seven categories.

Institutional Support. This category has three benchmarks related to the infrastructure that supports online course delivery: documented technology plans with security measures, guidelines for the reliability of the technology delivery system, and a centralized system of support for building and maintaining a distance education infrastructure. Whereas these benchmarks may seem obvious, of special interest were the two proposed standards that were not included in the final report. There is much discussion in higher education, in both academic and popular literature, about incentives and rewards for those involved, especially faculty. The two benchmarks, addressing incentives and rewards for faculty, were rejected in the final version of the paper as a result of the committee's belief that, in terms of incentives and rewards, distance education should not be treated differently from traditional classroom teaching.

Student Support. The benchmarks in this category provide information regarding programs, admission requirements, pricing, and the materials and technology that students will need to complete the courses. Additionally, three benchmarks describe requirements for hands-on training and information for students to access resources, specifics for technical assistance standards with quick and accurate responses to questions, and a structured system to address complaints. The understanding is that many students who take a distance education course will never visit a campus and will not use campus-based student support resources. At the same time, alternative forms of student support services are critical for the academic success of students and must be provided for students to succeed.

Faculty Support. The benchmarks in this category parallel those in the student support category. Faculty must have the opportunity to learn the skills needed to succeed in a distance-learning environment. However, the following questions were not resolved: To what extent are faculty members responsible for the development of an online course? What role should instructional designers play in this process? Are online courses best developed by a single faculty member or a team?

Course Development. The emphasis of this category is on the quality of the design of the courses, and it includes a requirement for a periodic review of instructional materials and minimum standards for course development, design, and delivery. This section also includes benchmarks that foster student engagement in the analysis, synthesis, and evaluation of the course material—elements that are commonly held as important for good instruction in general. Once again, the slate of benchmarks that did not make the cut is interesting to note. The literature on learning styles and the ability to customize learning styles to meet individual student needs is extensive. Several proposed benchmarks about student learning styles were rejected on the basis that these practices are not necessary to ensure quality. Other aspects of good pedagogy, such as interaction and constructive feedback, however, were seen as critical. Similarly, benchmarks that called for broad peer review and course design managed by teams were also dropped from the final listing. The study did reaffirm the responsibility of the instructor and the academic department for the development of courses, and, as noted above, reaffirmed that academic practices, such as peer review, should be the same for distance education and traditional courses.

Teaching and Learning Benchmarks. The benchmarks in this category pertain to the nature and quality of interactions between faculty and students. The benchmarks set standards for student and faculty interactions, as well as student-to-student interactions, and discuss the possibilities for new forms of communication using electronic media. Moreover, the benchmarks call for timely feedback to students, a welcome practice across higher education, and stress the importance of providing instruction to students on research methods. Rejected, but considered for the report, were measures to ensure quality practices in collaborative or group work.

Course Structure Benchmarks. The benchmarks in this category concern student preparedness in terms of motivation and technology, prior to taking an online course and other organizational issues once a course is in progress. These other issues include written course objectives and outcomes, access to library resources, and agreement about deadlines for assignments. The considerations that were examined for this segment of the project suggest that distance education is not for everyone. Knowing what to expect before electronic matriculation can reduce both anxiety and dropout rates. In other words, for quality distance education, students and faculty should be able to identify the objectives and projected outcomes before the course begins and then be able to evaluate whether or not the objectives were met and the outcomes were achieved.

Evaluation and Assessment. In the general discussion of distance education, both in the popular press and in the academy, this final category of benchmarks is perhaps one of the most controversial. Differing opinions about the learning effectiveness and cost effectiveness of distance education are defended with passion along with an appeal to evaluate and assess every aspect of the enterprise. The focus is on trying to determine whether the online educational program is effective, from both educational and financial perspectives. Thus, the benchmarks call for a multitiered evaluation process in which these variables are taken into account and data are collected and used to determine effectiveness. Finally, these benchmarks call for learning outcomes to be reviewed regularly with regard to clarity, utility, and appropriateness.

Quality on the Line presents an important schema for ensuring quality distance education. Given other perspectives highlighted in this chapter, however, it seems safe to conclude that *Quality on the Line* outlines benchmarks that are necessary but not sufficient to ensure quality. Other stakeholders have suggested quality benchmarks from their own perspectives. The benchmarks in the IHEP study focus on pedagogical and curricular issues. They are much less concerned with policy, institutionwide issues, and marketing considerations.

Accrediting Commissions

Accrediting commissions also provide perspectives on benchmarking in distance learning.

Statement of Commitment. One of the most significant indicators of any program in higher education is whether it is recognized by a regional or professional accrediting body. This is the case for measuring the quality of a distance education program as well. With eight regional accreditation associations in the United States[1], it is not unusual for them to have different approaches to accreditation and external review.

In the case of distance learning, however, each association was so pressed to develop benchmarks rapidly, the regional commissions worked together in an uncharacteristically unified move to craft benchmarking guidelines through the Council of Regional Accrediting Commissions. The first statement, "Statement of Commitment by the Regional Accrediting Commissions for the Evaluation of Electronically Offered Degree and Certificate Programs" (Council of Regional Accrediting Commissions, 2001b), is a "set of commitments aimed at ensuring high quality in distance education" (p. 1). Organized into three classifications, these commitments reflect common principles for the eight regional commissions.

Commitment to Traditions, Values, and Principles. The commissions assert that their history has been one of adapting to change and that responding to the growth of distance education is not a major departure from their basic educational philosophies. The commissions have recognized that their work in distance learning, will, by necessity, be a work in progress. They have acknowledged the importance of creating an effective balance between accountability and innovation. At the same time, the commissions explain that mission-driven standards have been and will continue to be used to define institutional quality. In other words, if innovations are too far removed from an institution's stated mission, it is likely that accrediting commissions will not easily approve these innovations.

This approach by the accrediting associations resulted in a resolution by the commissions to maintain traditional approaches in the development of standards. For example, they have indicated that higher education is best experienced in a community of learning, led by competent professionals. They also affirmed that student learning should be a dynamic and interactive process, regardless of the setting, and that substantive and coherent curricula are the organizing principles for degree programs. The commissions are committed especially to ensuring that institutions accept the obligation to address students' needs. They also, similar to the IHEP report, stressed the importance of evaluation, assessment, and quality improvement and, finally, encouraged institutions to voluntarily subject themselves to peer review.

Whereas the commissions' statement of commitment does not speak to the fact that these values are traditional and conservative, they do admit that there "are challenges in sustaining these important values through technologically mediated instruction" (Council of Regional Accrediting Commissions, 2001b, p. 3). This is especially evident because the commissions have also addressed course offerings provided by degree-granting institutions that do not necessarily lead to degrees, such as training and certificate programs. The commissions are also quite vocal when identifying some of the new partnerships and collaborative arrangements that higher education institutions are developing today. Their statement notes that the regional commissions consider it essential that accountability is fixed and expressed within the accredited institution. In other words, the accredited institution is responsible for the availability and provision of resources—even those that are beyond their control.

Commitment to Cooperation, Consistency, and Collaboration. The second category in the tripartite statement of commitment, while acknowledging the independence and autonomy of the regional commissions, is concerned with cross-regional consistency. This category highlights the fact that when institutions develop distance education programs leading to a degree for the first time, they will be subject to careful prior review. Institutional effectiveness in providing distance education will be "explicitly and rigorously appraised" as part of the regular evaluation (p. 4), and institutions are expected to conduct self-evaluation to improve their educational quality. Where deficiencies have been identified, the commissions expect remediation. In the extreme case, when an institution has been found to be incapable of offering distance education effectively, the commissions have agreed to take the appropriate action to remedy the situation (such as recommending the suspension of a program).

The final portion of the statement of commitment by the Council of Regional Accrediting Commissions is a companion document, "Best Practices for Electronically Offered Degree and Certificate Programs" (2001a). The regional commissions, through the Council of Regional Accrediting Commissions, contracted with the Western Cooperative for Educational Telecommunications to develop this detailed statement that is "a comprehensive and demanding expression of what is considered current best practice" (p. 5). This document provides guidelines for the myriad details related to the offering of distance education programs, including benchmarks for each area of activity and protocols that will assist administrators with both internal and external reviews.

Institutional Context and Commitment. The first component of "Best Practices," Institutional Context and Commitment, focuses on how distance education supports and extends the roles of institutions. Ten specific items flesh out the first component; they reflect concern about how distance education initiatives relate to an institution's mission and whether the institution has secured the resources necessary to support students in this new initiative. For example, there are questions about providing for a consistent, coherent, and appropriate technical framework, complete with support for students, as well as a check on an institution's understanding of and response to legal and regulatory requirements.

Curriculum and Instruction. The introduction to the second component, Curriculum and Instruction, notes that the important issues "are not technical but curriculum-driven and pedagogical" (p. 4). In this component, the focus is on appropriateness of curriculum developed by qualified professionals and on a coherent plan that enables students to complete a program. Another important consideration in this component is interaction between instructor and students and among students. Here, institutions are asked about provisions for interaction and the timeliness of instructor responses to students.

Faculty and Student Support. These two components share several aspects in common relative to the provision of adequate and appropriate technology support. The faculty support component also includes a review of personnel issues (compensation, workload, and intellectual property), with the expectation that an agreement with faculty covering these issues will have been completed prior to course development. As with the IHEP document, there is silence on the extensiveness of the faculty role in the development and delivery of distance education courses.

The student support section speaks to the services necessary to engage the student in the online course experience: assessment of readiness and advising, marketing information, full information about the course requirements and services, admissions, registration, and financial processes. The guidelines also address the support systems necessary for the student: library resources, tutoring, and bookstores. One subsection is somewhat unusual; it reflects the commissions' grounding in traditional academic values. This subsection emphasizes building a sense of community for distance education students through actions such as "encouraging study groups, providing student directories, including off-campus students in institutional publications and events, including these students in definitions of the academic community. . . invitations to campus events. . . and similar strategies of inclusion" (p. 12). What is interesting here is the silence about new technology strategies that are used and promoted to build community. Threaded discussion, chat rooms, and various e-mail services are standard fare in the portfolio of the major learning platform providers, in part to engender community among learners.

Evaluation and Assessment. The fifth and final component of the "Best Practices" document addresses assessment of student achievement and evaluation of the overall program in a setting that is evolving, where "the element of seat time is essentially removed from the equation" (p. 12). The commissions are looking to institutions to conduct "sustained, evidence-based and participatory inquiry as to whether distance learning programs are achieving objectives" (p. 12).

However, contemporary researchers suggest that such an approach may not go far enough. Olgren (1998) states that "to design effective distance education programs, it is important to understand how learning occurs and the factors that influence the learning process" (p. 77). She suggests that whereas the focus on learning outcomes in distance education is appropriate, it is incomplete. Olgren notes that learning for higher cognitive goals requires both analysis and synthesis. This suggests that course designers "will need to know more about their learners' cognitive strategies and prior knowledge in the content area" (p. 87). A better model, one that seeks to promote higher level goals of understanding and application, should include more than just pre-assessment of knowledge and skills. According to Olgren, information also needs to be gathered regarding students' "cognitive strategies, metacognitive strategies, and thinking skills" (p. 87).

Commission on Technology and Adult Learning. One factor that has contributed to the rapid expansion of distance education is the perception that it could effectively address workforce needs. In 2000, the American Society for Training and Development joined with the National Governors Association to define and encourage a technology-enabled learning environment. Achieved through the Commission on Technology and Adult Learning, which issued "A Vision of E-Learning for America's Workforce," the goal was to develop standards that would result in "an engaged citizenry and a skilled workforce for the digital economy" (Commission on Technology and Adult Learning, 2001, p. 2).

The Commission's Report

"A Vision of E-Learning" notes that the stakes are high for both the public and private sector. Specifically, the e-learning stakes for CEOs include the potential for gains in worker skills and productivity, cost savings, and access to high-quality training. Governors, too, have much to gain, as e-learning offers the potential for economic growth, better business performance, economic development at all levels, and improved lives for Americans. The report calls for concerted action, by the public and private sectors, especially in three major priority areas: quality, assessment and certification, and access.

The Quality Component. The commission has promulgated five specific recommendations relative to ensuring quality of e-learning. Undergirding the specific recommendations is an understanding that high-quality e-learning "provides just the right content at just the right time, helps learners master needed knowledge and skills, and draws people in so they are motivated to learn and apply their learning" (p. 18).

Critical of current quality assurance (QA), the commission noted that most of today's QA processes are "geographically rooted and focused on institutional providers" (p. 18). Moreover, these processes are "costly and slow. . . . rooted in utilization and completion rates rather than the added value or outcomes resulting from learning" (p. 18). These strategies don't work well in a context that is increasingly global, where the lines are blurred between traditional and new providers, and there is growing competition.

In response, the commission has called for greater emphasis on outcomes and public-private partnerships to conduct research on how adults learn and how to measure learning, to further our understanding of the best practices in technology-enabled content, delivery, and service. It is interesting to note the level of support for research in adult learning that is coming from the business and government sector. Researchers working in the field have called attention to the importance of this issue for distance education. Summarizing the best practices suggested by the various authors of her book, *Distance Learners in Higher Education,* Gibson (1998) highlights five components as critical. These include (1) know the learner; (2) provide orientations; (3) design with variety, active engagement, and choice; (4) evaluate authentically; and (5) provide an integrated system of support (pp. 140–142). In short, she concludes, "we, as distance educators, need to be learner-centered reflective practitioners" (p. 143).

The commission urges reliable and universally accessible consumer information about the quality of e-learning content, services and providers, learner outcomes, and customer satisfaction information (p. 20). This statement dramatically extends a priority expressed by the accrediting commissions, with serious implications for higher education administrators. Protection of student privacy and appropriate professional development for educators, especially in the area of adult learning, are benchmarks to enhance the quality of e-learning promoted by the commission.

Other Priority Areas. The remaining two priority areas in the report, assessment and access, though not explicitly concerned with ensuring the quality of e-learning, still have a direct impact on the quality of distance education. These include a call for broadening outcome measures and assessment tools, removing barriers to participation, and adopting technical standards that promote open and equitable access. The challenges for higher education administrators are significant. Workforce interests, as defended and promoted by business and government, are not necessarily assuaged by the standards of quality typically put forth by educational institutions and accrediting commissions. Rather, e-learning is viewed as a high-stakes adult learning initiative that has a direct impact on economic development and the quality of life for many communities. The vision statement suggests that using equivalency to on-campus learning as the measure of quality for e-learning is insufficient in today's technology-driven workplace; the high-tech demands of the workplace are requiring more high-tech solutions in the learning environment. Higher education administrators who wish to remain relevant in workforce education must harmonize these cutting-edge quality benchmarks with the more traditional and conservative academic context.

Supporting Teachers Through Benchmarks

A report by the American Federation of Teachers, "A Virtual Revolution: Trends in the Expansion of Distance Education" (2001), not unexpectedly makes a strong case for the role of professional teachers, noting that distance education can be a great asset as long as academic decision-making remains in the hands of teaching professionals. In contrast to other standards noted above, this report states, "serious problems arise if DE is organized primarily around corporate models of marketing and command-and-control management" (p. 3). Moreover, the report claims that much of the distance education reviewed is "built on corporate ideas about consumer focus, product standardization, tight personnel control and cost effectiveness" and it is stressed, "these concepts are contrary to the traditional model of higher education decision-making" (p. 4).

The report is critical of education based primarily on the marketplace and the model of the "student as customer," modularized courses, an unbundled faculty role, and standardization of coursework. Countering the standards outlined above, the AFT criticizes programs that rely on testing for individual outcomes and competencies while "downgrading the importance of class time and social interaction" (p. 4).

Driven by its philosophical stance, the AFT repeats fourteen benchmarks for achieving quality in the distance environment in this report, first published as "Guidelines for Good Practice" (2000). These standards include a strong role for faculty, such as retaining academic control, setting class size, retaining creative control over the use and re-use of materials, and "ensuring that faculty are in control of shaping and approving courses and integrating them into a coherent curriculum" (p. 20). Closely linked is a criticism of the movement toward a model of curriculum development and teaching that "unbundles" the many roles of the faculty member: "Students deserve teachers who know all the nuances of what they are teaching and who can exercise professional judgment and academic freedom in doing so" (p. 21).

Several other benchmarks reinforce other traditional aspects of higher education. For example, there is disagreement over the growing emphasis on outcomes rather than seat time: "The AFT, however, believes that deep knowledge of a subject is not simply a matter of passing a competency test" (p. 21). Furthermore, the AFT believes that seat time is important, noting, "distance education should utilize every available opportunity to bring students and faculty together at some time during an academic program" (p. 21). The benchmarks call for close personal interaction, comparable student assessment, and equivalent advisement opportunities. Like the other benchmarks already observed, these guidelines also call for evaluation of distance education coursework.

In closing, faculty are called to mobilize "behind the principle that democratic governance rather than top-down management produces better, more credible education" (p. 22). Unfortunately, the report treats this as an all-or-nothing situation. It is not. Also, the claims for "better, more credible education" are not substantiated and are vague enough to engender suspicion, even from a supportive audience. Finally, the AFT report observes that for higher education faculty to make distance education work, they may need to contradict current distance education practice to affirm academic values.

Major Agreement and Disagreement

A critical tour of the major published statements of benchmarks for distance education by various stakeholder groups is a necessary and illuminating exercise. As seen above, there is agreement among the various stakeholders on many issues. For example, there is general agreement that students need to be appropriately prepared and supported, and given adequate information about the technical and pedagogical requirements of an online course. There is also agreement that course objectives need to be clearly spelled out for students.

However, there is a lack of consensus among stakeholders about several aspects of the learning environment as it affects students. This includes the consideration of learning styles and, outside of the research community, little support for assessing learners' cognitive strategies and metacognitive strategies. There is disagreement over whether the use of collaborative or group work is an essential benchmark. There is also lack of consensus on the issue of time—time on task, seat time, response time. Finally, there is disagreement about how much the online learning environment should emulate the traditional classroom environment.

Likewise, there is consensus concerning faculty roles. There is agreement that faculty need support for the development of online learning. Most benchmarks agree that faculty contractual issues regarding compensation and intellectual property need to be addressed, though some reject these items as essential components to quality. There is perhaps stronger disagreement than consensus on other faculty issues, such as the level of involvement by faculty in controlling the design and construction of an online course. Whether or not instructional development teams are used remains an open issue for higher education administrators.

The Ideal Classroom?

The traditional classroom environment often used for comparison may be an idealized, even romanticized, standard. In their provocative article, Noone and Swenson (2001) make a strong case for new models of instruction in higher education. They challenge several traditionally held notions within the academy that have been used to critique distance education and to form benchmarks of quality that may in fact disadvantage distance education unfairly. They note that professors often know much about their discipline but little about teaching and even less about learning than teaching. They challenge the concept of "seat time," saying "inputs are easy to measure. . . . and so higher education clings to outdated measures like the Carnegie Unit as if they were articles of faith. . . . when we are concerned about how long a student's rear end is in a seat, we are concerned about the wrong end of the student" (p. 5).

There is consensus that more evaluation, summative and formative, needs to be undertaken for all distance education. There is disagreement, however, as to whether distance education should be subjected to more scrutiny than traditional classroom-based instruction. As already noted, researchers have called for greater attention to learning and the skills needed to foster more effective learning. And many of the principles identified by distance education proponents, such as a focus on learning styles, can be part of good pedagogy, independent of the course delivery method. In fact, there is reason to believe that some of the developments in distance learning may enhance traditional classroom instruction.

The expansion of distance education has come about quickly, in part due to rapid developments in technology and readily available popular access to the technology. Higher education has been challenged, at best, and overwhelmed, at worst, in trying to keep up with new developments, new providers, new models, and new methods. In response to calls for quality assurance, various benchmarks have been developed that are probably best viewed as temporary measures. The educational demands of the future, especially relative to workforce needs, will not be satisfied by yesterday's solutions. Likewise, benchmarks developed for today will need to be constantly reviewed for appropriateness and modified as needed. The challenge for all higher education administrators is to determine how to remain part of this ongoing process effectively as they enter this constantly changing new world.

Note

1. The eight regional accrediting commissions are as follows:

- Commission on Higher Education, Middle States Association of Colleges and Schools
- Commission on Institutions of Higher Education, New England Association of Schools and Colleges
- Commission on Technical and Career Institutions, New England Association of Schools and Colleges
- Commission on Institutions of Higher Education, North Central Association of Colleges and Schools
- Commission on Colleges, The Northwest Association of Schools and Colleges
- Commission on Colleges, Southern Association of Colleges and Schools
- Accrediting Commission for Community and Junior Colleges, Western Association of Schools and Colleges
- Accrediting Commission for Senior Colleges and Universities, Western Association of Schools and Colleges

References

American Federation of Teachers. "Distance Education: Guidelines for Good Practice." [http://www.aft.org/higher_ed/downloadable/distance.pdf]. 2000.

American Federation of Teachers. "A Virtual Revolution: Trends in the Expansion of Distance Education." [http://www.aft.org/higher_ed/downloadable/Virtual Revolution.pdf]. 2001.

Commission on Technology and Adult Learning. "A Vision of E-Learning for America's Workforce." [http://www.nga.org/cda/files/ELEARNINGREPORT.pdf]. July 2001.

Council of Regional Accrediting Commissions. "Best Practices for Electronically Offered Degree and Certificate Programs." [http://www.wiche.edu/telecom/Accrediting—BestPractices.pdf]. June 2001a.

Council of Regional Accrediting Commissions. "Statement of Commitment by the Regional Accrediting Commissions for the Evaluation of Electronically Offered Degree and Certificate Programs." [http://www.wiche.edu/telecom/Accrediting—Commitment.pdf]. June 2001b.

Gibson, C. C. (ed.). *Distance Learners in Higher Education: Institutional Responses for Quality Outcomes.* Madison, Wis.: Atwood, 1998.

Institute for Higher Education Policy. "Quality on the Line: Benchmarks for Success in Internet-Based Distance Education." [http://www.ihep.com/Pubs/PDF/Quality.pdf]. 2000.

Noone, L. P., and Swenson, C. "Five Dirty Little Secrets in Higher Education." In *Educause Review,* [http://www.educause.edu/pub/er/erm01/erm016w.html]. Dec. 2001.

Olgren, C. H. "Improving Learning Outcomes: The Effects of Learning Strategies and Motivation." In C. Campbell (ed.), *Distance Learners in Higher Education: Institutional Responses for Quality Outcomes.* Madison, Wis.: Atwood, 1998.

Russell, T. L. *No Significant Difference Phenomenon.* Raleigh: North Carolina State University Press, 1999.

Verduin, J. R., Jr., and Clark, T. A. *Distance Education: The Foundations of Effective Practice.* San Francisco: Jossey-Bass, 1991.

RICHARD J. NOVAK *is executive director for continuous education and distance learning at Rutgers, The State University of New Jersey.*

6

Benchmarking provides increasingly useful information for state higher education boards. This chapter provides information on how boards use benchmarking in their operations.

Benchmarking by State Higher Education Boards

Robert J. Barak, Charles R. Kniker

What is benchmarking? In the narrowest sense, it is an organization's comparison with the best practice established by another entity, sometimes in a different field, that is used to improve, in the case of higher education, a process, procedure, or outcome. For proponents of this perspective, benchmarking is gaining numbers within an organization or between organizations for the sake of comparison (Alstete, 1995).

For others, however, the term *benchmarking* describes a wide array of management practices by state higher education boards (used here to encompass both statewide coordinating and governing boards and multi-campus system governing boards). Bogan and English (1994, pp. 7–8) have identified three types of benchmarking that largely explain this array of activities. The three types include: (1) performance benchmarking, (2) strategic benchmarking, and (3) process benchmarking. *Performance benchmarking* generally focuses on specific issues such as quality and performance characteristics. *Strategic benchmarking* refers to fundamental lessons and winning strategies. *Process benchmarking* focuses on distinct work processes and operating systems and attempts to identify the most effective operating practices that can result in performance improvements. These performance improvements may be measured through increased productivity and lower operating costs. Whereas the bulk of the activity by state boards has focused on performance benchmarking, there are notable gains in the other two areas as well. This chapter concerns the way state higher education boards use information generated by benchmarking processes. It also describes how one state governing board uses benchmarks in working with its institutions and includes indicators used by selected state higher education boards.

States' Use of Performance Benchmarking

In 1998, Christal reported that thirty-seven states used performance measures (Christal, 1998). This number was more than double the number using performance measures in a study just three years earlier. In addition, seven additional states reported that they were developing performance measures. The major objectives noted by the state higher education boards in the use of performance measures were to improve institutional performance, enhance undergraduate education, and increase institutional accountability. Legislators and governors either mandated most of the performance measures for accountability or were heavily involved in their development.

The accountability aspect of performance measures is perhaps the most unusual use among all the various entities using performance measures for benchmarking. These performance indicators are frequently used to provide a form of consumer protection for the public, which is often is defined as students and parents. Typically, the consumer reporting is made in the form of a consumer guide or report card.

Perhaps the most sophisticated use of the performance measures is in the budgeting process. According to Christal, eight states directly link the performance measures with the budget process whereas another fifteen consider the performance measures in allocating resources. In another study, Albright (1998) found that more than half the states (thirty-two) were planning to or using performance measures in their state budgeting process. Albright noted that performance funding was being used to "eliminate programs; reduce the size of programs; focus on outcomes rather than inputs; clarify state priorities; emphasize important educational goals; link budgeting with planning and programming; and encourage change" (p. 11).

According to Albright, the twelve most commonly reported performance measures in the states surveyed are as follows:

- Retention or graduation rates
- Program delivery, such as improving access, range, efficiency, expediency, or transferability
- Assessment processes and results
- Workforce development
- Student characteristics and student diversity or faculty and staff diversity
- Alumni, enrolled students, or employer survey results
- Mission-specific objectives
- Administrative efficiencies
- Accreditation
- Linkages with elementary through high school
- Affordable tuition and fees
- Institutional program review and improvement

Strategic benchmarking influences the longer-term competitive patterns of an organization. These benchmarks focus on fundamental lessons and winning strategies. Whereas the competitive aspect as noted by Bogan and English is perhaps less important to state higher education boards, several boards conduct benchmarking-type activities that reflect a long-term perspective. The board of regents in Iowa, for example, combines strategic planning, budgeting, and performance outcomes that focus on long-term systemic improvements at the institutions.

According to Bogan and English, process benchmarking focuses on discrete work processes and operating systems. This form of benchmarking seeks to identify the most efficient and effective institutional practices. For example, the board of regents in Iowa periodically conducts organizational audits, which focus on such areas as purchasing processes, strategic planning, and various administrative practices. Practices and processes frequently are compared with others in the field. The goal here is to improve core processes, which in turn can result in performance improvements for users of institutional services.

Our informal survey of state boards in early 2001 concluded that many states use various types of performance indicators, which may or may not be tied to funding. State boards have multiple reasons for using evaluation techniques other than benchmarking, although there are some indications that benchmarking is on the increase. Selected reasons for not adopting benchmarking include, first, the commitment of state boards to long-range planning and strategic planning. Second, institutional research offices at smaller institutions are often understaffed, as are most state board offices. Third, despite the information available from Integrated Postsecondary Educational Data System, and a variety of other national databases, institutions that are currently making peer comparisons express frustration at the limited compatibility of such data. Higher education peers seldom have truly similar departmental and collegiate structures, budgets, or student bodies. It is difficult for state higher education boards to gain insights when peer data reports change periodically.

Consumer demand, backed by federal legislation (Higher Education Act of 1998), has forced universities and colleges to make more knowledge public. For example, campus crime statistics, financial aid funding rates, and percentages of students participating in intercollegiate athletics are published regularly.

Whereas the public wants more accountability from state higher education institutions, the percentage of state appropriations that public institutions receive is declining. A growing percentage of funding is private contributions. Whether individual philanthropists or corporate leaders, these donors are another constituent group that wants to see evidence of institutions practicing effective management.

Our survey in early 2000 supports Christal's findings, previously noted. We found that respondents' performance measures reflected those categories that are most popular. That list is similar to the top ten identified by Taylor and Massey (1996).

Our review included the following state boards of higher education. We believe it is important to note which are governing boards and which are coordinating boards. The governing boards are Arizona, Hawaii, North Carolina, and Utah. The coordinating boards are California, Missouri, New Jersey, Ohio, Oklahoma, South Carolina, Tennessee, Texas, and Virginia.

The generalizations from these thirteen state higher education boards and Iowa include the following:

- Indicators are quantitative (numbers, ratios, percentages) and often are included in past or developing strategic plans. Typically, the performance indicators have targets.
- There is a trend toward greater use of performance processes. One example would be studies of students' perceptions of the advising received over time (National Survey of Student Engagement, 2000).
- There is greater use of peer benchmarking. A caution raised is that the peer institution or system may have established a goal that was relatively easy to achieve in light of its unique circumstance.

A distant cousin to benchmarking is the use of ratings. One type of rating is a report card. Some either mirror the National Center for Public Policy and Higher Education's *Measuring Up 2000,* in which all states were graded on preparation, participation, affordability, completion, benefits, and learning. (Norma Salas of the Arizona Board of Regents has prepared a helpful summary based on a national survey of such report cards and accountability reports.) Other types of rating are either media or private-sector articles that base their comparative ratings on specific criteria (Lombardi Program for Measuring University Performance, 2000; Feemster, 2000; Morse and Flanigan 2000).

In the states surveyed, as well as those reported in the literature, funding related to performance is increasing. Tennessee stated that it was the first state to have used financial incentives to have its institutions improve the quality of instruction. South Carolina claims that its funding targets are institution-specific. However, in South Carolina, the practice includes similar targets for specific sectors, such as research universities and technical schools.

The recommendations and caveats include the following:[1]

- Keep the list of performance benchmarks to as few as possible.
- There is no short list that can apply to all institutions equally. The mission, size, history, and specific culture and environment of institutions within a system determine those indicators that will be most appropriate.

- Advocates claim that indicators promote analysis for institutional improvement.
- The critics contend that performance benchmarks cannot adequately measure important intangibles such as quality of instruction and quality of campus spirit.
- Critics believe that indicators are inappropriately used to assess faculty performance or to eliminate programs.

A Case Study

The remainder of this segment of the chapter blends a case study of the actions taken by the Board of Regents, State of Iowa (a governing board), with similar performance benchmarks that are in force or proposed in other states. The purpose of this section is to show how a governing board is attempting to be responsible in reporting the activities of its three universities to the public, over time, while being sensitive to pressures to add benchmarks.

In 1998, the board adopted a new five-year plan that included four key result areas (KRAs)—quality, access, diversity, and accountability. Each KRA (the board chose not to call them goals) had objectives, strategies, and action steps. Each action step identified who was responsible (such as the board, the executive director of the board, the institutional presidents, or others) for successfully completing the action step. A time line was included, plus a column indicating how the outcome, if ongoing, would be monitored. In some cases, the monitoring would be through an annual report to the board; in other cases, by development of specific presentations or special reports.

In addition to having a strategic plan for the Iowa State Board, the regents required that each of its institutions also have a five-year plan. Furthermore, the board mandated that there would be an annual progress report on achieving the institutional goals. The individual strategic plans contained some performance indicators. The board also determined that it wanted some of the annual governance reports to include indicators. At its December 1998 meeting, the board formally adopted forty-three performance indicators that were to be included in an annual report the following December.

During the ensuing year, a work group of representatives from the regent institutions and the board office met to clarify criteria and parameters of the indicators. In some cases, the work group made allowances for individual institutional differences; in other cases, each of the five institutions had to report on the same indicator. Another important change the work group recommended to the board was that a clear distinction be made between some indicators that were clearly focused on a performance that had or could have a target and those indicators that were indicated as monitoring tools. For the latter category, the work group proposed the term *common data sets.* In the December 1999 report on performance indicators, the forty-three indicators were clustered under four categories: twelve common data sets applied to all five institutions, another ten were common for the three universities, two related to just the two special schools, and the remainder were linked to one or two of the universities.

During the following year, the work group recommended one additional change. It organized the common data sets and performance indicators under six headings that it believed would be logical to the board and the public. The six headings were instructional environment; student profile and performance; educational outreach and service; faculty profile and productivity; diversity; and expenditures, financing, and funding. Additional refinements made for the December 2000 report to the board were presentations of five years or more of data for each of the forty-three indicators or common data sets in statistical and chart format.

Following are the six areas, with performance indicators and common data sets, reported in December 2000.

• *Instructional environment.* Average undergraduate class size (all); number and percentage of general assignment technology-equipped classrooms (all); percentage of course sections using computers as an integral teaching aid (all); percentage of undergraduate student credit hours taught by tenured or tenure track faculty (universities); percentage of senior faculty teaching undergraduates (State University of Iowa [SUI]); number, total, and percentage of faculty using instructional technology (SUI, University of Northern Iowa [UNI]); percentage of introductory course taught by senior faculty (Iowa State University [ISU]); percentage of lower division courses taught by tenured or tenure track faculty (UNI); percentage of senior faculty teaching at least one undergraduate course annually (ISU); and percentage of faculty who use computers as a teaching aid (ISU).

• *Student profile and performance.* Fall enrollment, by level, age, and residency; undergraduate student retention and graduation rates (all); percentage of professional students passing licensure examinations (SUI and ISU); percentage of all [undergraduate] graduates employed within one year (universities); average Graduate Record Exam (GRE) composite score of entering graduate students (SUI).

• *Educational service and outreach.* Headcount enrollments in credit and noncredit courses (universities); off-campus student enrollment in degree programs (universities); number of nondegree enrollments (SUI); availability of off-campus credit courses (UNI); number of extension clients (ISU); number of Iowa Communications Network (ICN) sites served by Hancher [Fine Arts Center] Programming (SUI); number of annual visits to the University of Iowa Health Sciences Centers (SUI).

• *Faculty profile and performance.* Faculty resignations, retirements, and new hires (all); sponsored funding per year (universities); number of intellectual property disclosures (universities); annual publication indices (SUI); annual citation indices (SUI); number of external funding proposals submitted (SUI); percentage of faculty with one scholarly work published during last three academic years (ISU); percentage of faculty as principal or coprincipal investigators (ISU); sponsored funding per faculty member (ISU); number of new technologies licensed (ISU); number of new technologies generating revenues and amount of total revenues (ISU); number of external grants and contracts awarded (ISU).

- *Institutional diversity.* Racial or ethnic composition of student, faculty, and staff populations, in percentages (all).
- *Expenditures, financing, and funding.* State appropriations requested (all); number of annual contributors and dollar value of contributions (all); amount of capital improvement funds requested and appropriated (all); deferred maintenance (all); percentage of resources reallocated annually (all); growth in undergraduate tuition and fees, related to HEPI (universities); number and dollars in millions of financial aid received by resident undergraduates and percentage of need met (universities); unit cost per student (universities).

After the December 2000 board meeting, some board members and staff of the board office wondered if indicators used in other states might be added or substituted for some of the original indicators. That interest prompted the informal study previously mentioned. What we concluded from printed documents and telephone interviews with representatives of other state higher education boards is that benchmarking, in the narrowest sense of the definition by Bogan and English, is not widely used, for the reasons stated. Several annual governance documents presented to the board, such as the Faculty Activities report (workload and productivity), incorporate data on student credit hours by faculty rank at peer institutions.

Table 6.1 is a sample of indicators other states use that are different from the ones used in Iowa. They are compiled using the six categories the Board of Regents, State of Iowa used.

What trends can be discerned, especially concerning the use of benchmarking rather than performance indicators? We have identified three trends:

- The first is toward greater use of performance *processes* to supplement performance outcomes measures. A national study on student engagement has had some influence on this.
- A second trend is the use of, or consideration of, *performance funding.*
- *Benchmarking* is the third trend. One state, South Carolina, encourages its higher education institutions to have several sets of peers. One peer group would be the best in practice cluster. Another set of peer institutions would be institutions that are at a slightly higher level of performance. Pragmatically, that group would be used for incremental improvements.

We would like to make a final comment about state higher education boards' indirect use of ratings. Whether the ratings are published in *U.S.*

Table 6.1. Additional Indicators

Instructional Environment
Percentage of courses by course level with less than twenty and more than fifty students
(Virginia)
Percentage of lower division students with two or more classes taught by regular faculty and
percentage with one or no classes (Hawaii)
Percentage of graduate students and upper division undergraduate students participating in
sponsored research program (South Carolina)
Percentage of programs eligible for specialized or professional accreditation that hold such
accreditation (Virginia and Missouri)
Percentage of degree or certificate programs that have a required practice or service-related
component (Hawaii)

Student Profile and Performance
Headcount enrollments (virtually every state, many including breakdowns of data showing
resident and non-resident ratios, transfer numbers of community college and private college
students)
Percentages of freshman applications, accepted, and actual enrollees (North Carolina, and
several other states)
Percentage of top high school students (top 10 percent) who attend a public university
(Arizona)
Number or percentage of transfer students to four-year institutions and their retention and
graduation rates (Virginia, Hawaii, Arizona, South Carolina, North Carolina)
Success of students who complete remediation courses in English and math (Ohio, South
Carolina)
Annualized salaries of graduates by discipline (Ohio, West Virginia)
Satisfaction with institution, by graduates and employers of graduates (Hawaii, South Carolina)
Percentage of teacher education graduates in state-identified critical shortage areas (South
Carolina)

Educational Outreach and Service
Calculating costs of incremental distance education expenditures (Iowa)

Faculty Profile and Performance
Percentage of faculty with good or excellent teaching ratings (Hawaii)
Percentage of students "satisfied or above" with advisor availability (South Carolina)

Institutional Diversity
Respect for differences (based on student survey) (Hawaii)
Number and percentage of international students (Hawaii)
Percentage of students who participate in study-abroad programs (Iowa)

Expenditures, Financing, and Funding
Debt service to revenue ratio (Virginia)
Percentage of living alumni that contribute in a given year (Virginia)
Proportion of state operating budget used for educational activities (Arizona)
Percentage of administrative expenditures to academic expenditures

News & World Report, the more recent *The Lombardi Program on Measuring University Performance,* or some reputed study, institutional leaders and state board members certainly are aware of them. If the ratings are high, trustees and regents will hear the voices of presidents and public relations officials. If the ratings are lower than expected, the same voices speak of questionable data and flawed methodology. Interestingly, a trend that we noticed our research universities developed was to include indicators and targets related to faculty membership in learned societies, the number of prestigious awards, or citations in select publications. Rather than playing the ratings game, some of these may be viewed as an indirect way to benchmark.

Conclusion

State higher education boards face a daunting task of providing meaningful accountability measures. Boards are expected to please a variety of constituent groups whose bottom lines are different. The task of state boards is compounded by the range of institutions they govern or coordinate, from comprehensive regional campuses to research universities. As noted in this chapter, performance indicators and common data sets are much more likely to be found than benchmarking. Benchmarking, if its advocates are accurate, may be viewed by faculty and campus administration as more compatible to their missions (which often include phrases about excellence in teaching, research, and service) and less benign than the quantitative "bean-counting" indicators.

Universities' and boards' resistance to benchmarking will be reduced when they are convinced that valid and reliable data can be obtained.

Note

1. The following documents were used to develop the list of generalizations, recommendations, and caveats:

Arizona Board of Regents. "Arizona University System: 2000 Report Card."

California Postsecondary Education Commission. "Performance Indicators of California Higher Education." 2000.

Missouri Department of Higher Education. "Show-Me Higher Education. . . . Ensuring Access, Quality, and Efficiency." 1998 Annual Report.

New Jersey Commission on Higher Education. "Accountability in Higher Education: The Fourth Annual System-wide Report." 2000.

Oklahoma State Regents for Higher Education. "A Focus on Higher Education in Oklahoma." 2000.

South Carolina Commission on Higher Education. "A Closer Look at Public Higher Education in South Carolina—Institutional Effectiveness, Accountability, and Performance." 2000.

State Council of Higher Education for Virginia. "SCHEV Approves 14 Performance Measures for 4-Year Public Colleges." Nov. 21, 2000 (News release).

Tennessee Higher Education Commission. "Biennial Report of the Tennessee Higher Education Commission for 1995–1998."

University of Hawaii. "Benchmarks/Performance Indicators Report." 2000.

University of North Carolina, Chapel Hill. "Statistical Abstract of Higher Education in North Carolina, 1999–2000." 2000.

Utah System of Higher Education. "Highlights of the Utah System of Higher Education Master Plan 2000: A Commitment to the People of Utah." 2000.

References

Albright, B. N. *The Transition from Business as Usual to Funding for Results: State Efforts to Integrate Performance Measures in the Higher Education Budgetary Process.* Denver: State Higher Education Executive Officers, 1998.

Alstete, J. W. *Benchmarking in Higher Education: Adapting Best Practices to Improve Quality.* ASHE-ERIC Higher Education Report, no. 5. San Francisco: Jossey-Bass, 1995.

Bogan, C. E., and English, M. J. *Benchmarking for Best Practices: Winning Through Innovative Adaptation.* New York: McGraw-Hill, 1994.

Christal, M. E. *State Survey on Performance Measures: 1996–97.* Denver: State Higher Education Executive Officers, 1998.

Feemster, R. "By the Numbers: Diversity Index." *University Business*, 2000, *79*, 27–28.

Lombardi Program for Measuring University Performance. "The Top American Research Universities." Occasional paper, July 2000.

Morse, R. J., and Flanigan, S. M. "How We Rank the Colleges." *U.S. News & World Report*, Sept. 11, 2000.

National Survey of Student Engagement. "National Benchmarks of Effective Educational Practice." Nov. 2000.

"Successful Companies Change the Rules of the Game." *Human Resource Management News*, Apr. 15, 2000, *50*(8).

Taylor, B. E., and Massy, W. F. *Strategic Indicators for Higher Education, 1996.* Princeton, N.J.: Peterson's, 1996.

ROBERT J. BARAK *is associate executive director, Iowa Board of Regents.*

CHARLES R. KNIKER *is associate director, academic affairs, Iowa Board of Regents.*

7

This chapter provides an overview of benchmarking in student affairs and provides several case studies that demonstrate how benchmarking has been used in student housing.

Benchmarking in Student Affairs

Robert E. Mosier, Gary J. Schwarzmueller

Because of rapid technological changes, the fluctuating economy, a reduction in support from states and the federal government, changing demographics, and the attitudes of potential students as customers with new needs and changing demands, many higher education institutions are experiencing the same uncertainties that businesses are.

Because of this uncertainty, student affairs and student housing have placed a strong emphasis on improving the efficiency, effectiveness, and accountability of the education that students receive at colleges and universities. This focus is also a result of oversight by state legislatures, regional accrediting agencies, boards of trustees, and other groups. Regional accrediting agencies have asked colleges and universities to (1) develop clear goals stated in terms of outcomes, (2) develop measures to demonstrate goal achievement, and (3) demonstrate that the results of the measures have been used to guide improvements.

Implied in this assessment process is the need to demonstrate effectiveness through best practices and to show through outcomes measurement that value has been added to the students' education.

Another significant influence on the educational and administrative policies and procedures of colleges and universities has been the adaptation of corporate and business practices. Management by objectives (MBO), total quality management (TQM), continuous quality improvement (CQI), strategic planning, environmental scanning, quality circles, and benchmarking have had varying degrees of success in higher education. Examples of concepts that have received fairly widespread acceptance and common use include program reviews, market profiling and segmentation, and enrollment management. This chapter describes the benchmarking process as it applies to student affairs in general and student housing. Institutional examples will be provided to illustrate the application of benchmarking in specific situations.

The Benchmarking Process

As managers in higher education face multiple business approaches, the question becomes how to select a process that can be most beneficial. Benchmarking is gaining increasing support in higher education because of its ability to improve the students' educational experiences. Epper (1999) views benchmarking as involving three key components: (1) examining and understanding one's internal work procedures, (2) searching for best practices in other organizations that match with one's own program, and (3) adapting those practices to improve performance.

The benchmarking practitioner needs to focus on two areas: performance benchmarking (looking at comparable outcome data with other schools) and process benchmarking (examining one's own internal processes that impact on outcomes). According to Epper, one of the most useful tools for dealing with the current competition and uncertainty in higher education is that of process benchmarking. Focusing inwardly on one's own processes can lead to major changes.

With respect to approaches to benchmarking, Alstete (1995) describes four types of benchmarking: internal benchmarking, competitive benchmarking, functional benchmarking, and generic benchmarking. Internal benchmarking involves making comparisons within an organization, whereas competitive benchmarking examines performance against peer or competitor organizations. Within competitive benchmarking, it is common for a third party or outside organization to conduct the research. Examples of this would be studies conducted by associations such as the National Association of College and University Business Officers (NACUBO) or private consulting firms such as Educational Benchmarking Incorporated (EBI). Functional, or industry benchmarking, involves looking at high performing processes industrywide. Lastly, generic, or best-in-class benchmarking, looks at organizations outside of one's field or industry, making comparisons at times between very different organizations. In the area of marketing, for example, a student housing organization might compare itself to the practices of Disney World.

Benchmarking Within Student Affairs

As in other areas of higher education, benchmarking practices in student affairs accelerated during the 1990s. The changes have occurred primarily through the coordination of professional associations such as NACUBO, the National Association of College and University Food Services (NACUFS), and the Association of College and University Housing Officers-International (ACUHO-I). Whereas some institutions such as Oregon State University and Babson College have conducted individual benchmarking surveys, the coordinated efforts of professional associations has led to more comprehensive comparative surveys between institutions.

The NACUBO Benchmarking Project. NACUBO began its most recent benchmarking efforts in 1991, when it developed a pilot study involving more than sixteen hundred individuals on forty campuses. Benchmarks were designed in forty topical areas. Based on user feedback, the number of benchmarks has since been cut back to twenty-six core functional areas, including admissions, bookstores, financial aid, food services, registration and records, student health services, and student housing. NACUBO received assistance from the Higher Education Consulting Group of Coopers and Lybrand and three other consulting firms. As an example of the type of data that would be received from the benchmarking survey in admissions, an institution could gain benchmarks about the median offers of admission as a percentage of applicants, the average number of secondary school graduates as a percentage of acceptances, and the average number of calendar days required to process an application.

A comprehensive study involving all twenty campuses of the California State University system was carried out in 1993 using the NACUBO benchmarking process (Alstete, 1995). Among the student affairs topics covered were admissions, financial aid, and registration and records. Comparisons were made with institutions both within and outside of the California State University system. Generally, participation in the study was viewed as valuable, with positive changes occurring in practices and procedures (Alstete, 1995).

NACUBO maintains an effective practices database, which contains information about effective practices and cost-saving measures from various colleges and universities across the country. In addition, NACUBO develops forums to address issues of continuous quality improvement on campuses.

The NACUFS Benchmarking Project. NACUFS has developed and maintains the Operating Performance Benchmarking Survey for food services and dining operations across the country. Designed to complement this survey is the Customer Satisfaction Benchmarking Survey. This instrument allows food service programs to survey students who use residential dining halls and retail facilities. The results of the survey can be used to compare customer satisfaction with national benchmarks. The instrument measures satisfaction with food, service, and the dining environment.

Another benchmarking survey provided by NACUFS is the Commodity Basket Service. This instrument provides a quarterly measurement of prices paid for thirty-six of the most commonly purchased foods for colleges and universities. The results indicate whether the prices being paid by the colleges' food service program are between the twenty-fifth and seventy-fifth percentiles. This helps food service directors and others see how competitive their prices are compared with other institutions.

Examples of Benchmarking Projects in Student Affairs. Oregon State University carried out a major benchmarking project in the early 1990s in which it compared itself to eight other universities. One of the areas it examined was student services, including admissions and recruitment. The university received comparative data on factors such as the average number of days from completed application to decision mailed and the average number of days of the receipt of inquiry to the first response. The institution was able to find out how effective it was relative to the other schools (Alstete, 1995).

Babson College engaged in a generic benchmarking project in which it compared itself to organizations outside of higher education. Babson met with representatives from hotels for their registration and check-in processes, Disney Corporation representatives for their technology advances, banks for their billing processes, and an accounting firm for its use of technology in recruitment. Babson found the businesses to be very responsive and helpful.

Benchmarking Within Student Housing

Housing programs have always been very visible on campus because they support the academic mission; provide clean, safe, affordable accommodations; are financially self-supporting; and meet the ever increasing needs and wants of parents and students. Most institutions have a pressing need for new housing and substantial renovation of existing housing. Additions and upgrades are needed to support the latest in communication technologies, to meet all new safety and accessibility codes, and to offer market grade amenities. Students, parents, faculty, and various campus staff members are all stakeholders in the housing program. The large stakeholder group provides extra motivation for housing professionals to have continuous improvement and customer service programs in place.

One of the primary responsibilities of the ACUHO-I executive board is to listen regularly to its members, identify member needs, and provide products and services that meet those needs. Members often have expressed needs for comparative information with other housing programs in higher education and for the identification of effective practices in residential programs. In the mid-1990s the executive board reviewed some benchmarking studies conducted by other higher education associations and concluded that ACUHO-I did not have the expertise or other resources required to properly conduct benchmarking studies for its members at that time. This was a very uncomfortable position for the board but an accurate reflection of the situation.

In the spring of 1997, representatives from a company that specializes in higher education benchmarking, EBI, proposed a partnership with

ACUHO-I to provide benchmarking studies for housing professionals. The proposal was promising enough to the board that focus groups were conducted at the summer 1997 ACUHO-I annual conference to ascertain if there was member interest. Members were enthusiastic about the prospect of having benchmarking services specifically designed for housing and residence life operations.

Several points were made clear during the focus groups. Most participants said they would participate in an ACUHO-I benchmarking program. It was acceptable for ACUHO-I to develop a partnership with a for-profit company, but it was critical that housing practitioners identify the studies that were needed, define terms, and play the major role in content development. They also wanted to participate in studies through ACUHO-I with payments made to the association. In short, they wanted assurance that this was an ACUHO-I program with significant practitioner involvement.

The executive board reviewed the results of the focus groups and decided to enter into a formal partnership with the company. A group of members was identified to begin working with the company to plan for the initial studies. The benchmarking group became a strategic planning task force within the association's governance structure.

The executive board and the five strategic planning task force chairs met with a consultant in Chicago in October 1997. Several important concepts were discussed at the meeting which changed ACUHO-I's approach to the benchmarking project. The need to become more flexible and get new products and services into members' hands more quickly was made very clear. ACUHO-I was advised to separate product development from the governance process. The implication for the benchmarking project was changing the benchmarking group from a strategic planning task force to a product development team (PDT) with a short, focused goal. The executive board set expected outcomes and operational limits and assigned these tasks to the executive director, the association treasurer, and the PDT chair. Periodic reports were expected, but the board did not need to get involved in the details of accomplishing the task.

After the October 1997 meeting, work proceeded on two fronts. The executive director and principals in the company negotiated a contract that was signed in January 1998. Simultaneously, the PDT began working with the company to decide which studies were needed and in what order. Two types of studies were planned: satisfaction studies and studies of administrative practices. Given the emphasis on getting products to the members quickly, it was decided that the satisfaction studies would be done first, as that type of study was familiar to most on the PDT and to the company.

A resident satisfaction study was the first developed, and it was offered during winter and spring 1998. Results were available just prior to the annual conference in July 1998. ACUHO-I met its goal of putting the benchmarking surveys in members' hands quickly: it took less than a year from the board's initial concept discussion for members to begin using the benchmarking surveys. Once focus groups ascertained probable program value, it took a year before an analysis of first-year survey results was completed. The benchmarking PDT accomplished its mission of assisting in bringing this first study into being. It was clear that continual input from a similar group would be required to develop other studies. A benchmarking services team was charged with the responsibility of working with the company and developing new studies.

A study of resident assistant satisfaction was added the second year. This, too, was well received by members. Many improvements in structuring the resident assistant experience have resulted. During the first and second years of offering the resident satisfaction studies, members requested a wide variety of additional types of reports and analyses. Many new types of reports, analyses, and other program enhancements were offered based on input from users. One strength of the program is the continuing interaction among those using the services—the benchmarking services team and the company.

As the program grew and additional studies were envisioned, the company and ACUHO-I jointly made the decision to hire a consultant to provide assistance with three critical services:

- Listening to current and potential users and identifying their needs
- Marketing all the studies to potential users
- Helping participants in the studies use the results to make improvements in their housing programs

The first chairman of the ACUHO-I benchmarking services team retired from his housing position and became the first consultant to fill this position.

In the third year, a satisfaction study for apartments was offered. User feedback had revealed that the living experience of residence hall and apartment residents was different enough to warrant separate studies for each. This third study was well received by members.

As the initial contract neared completion, the ACUHO-I executive director and principals from the company evaluated the experience and identified several areas in which the contract could be improved. A new three-year contract was signed effective July 1, 2000.

The need for a study of administrative practices was identified early in the planning process. It was clear from the start that this study would be more complex and challenging than the satisfaction studies. After about two years of preparation, an administrative study was offered in 2000. The study was comprehensive and included well-defined terms, but housing administrators were challenged by the high volume of information requested and the fact that information was requested about areas often not under the control of survey respondents. The company then had to present the large volume of information in ways that were both meaningful and easy to comprehend and use. The conclusion reached after evaluating the first administrative study was that too much information was requested and that the results were too extensive and complex to be used easily by participants. After extensive review, the decision was made to concentrate on a much smaller list of items critical to housing personnel and to correlate these administrative practices with resident satisfaction.

Information from the studies has been shared with the membership through sessions at the ACUHO-I annual conference and at regional conferences; through articles in the ACUHO-I newsmagazine, the *Talking Stick*; and on the ACUHO-I and company World Wide Web sites. A workshop was also held that helped participants understand and use the results.

Several lessons are evident after reviewing the evolution of ACUHO-I's benchmarking program:

- The availability of a for-profit partner with economic incentives to invest in instrument and report development was necessary for the project to move quickly from the "discovery of need" stage to the "delivery of product" stage.
- A key to the program's success has been continual listening to and responding to user feedback.
- Having college housing practitioners fully involved in product design and review ensured that the products would meet member needs and also that members would be comfortable enrolling in the studies.
- New and improved products would not have been available in as timely a fashion if the executive board had not authorized the executive director and a few volunteer leaders to make decisions and move the project forward.
- The relationship between the association and the company is dynamic and requires regular attention. If it doesn't receive enough attention, minor differences of opinion will become major problems. Regular communication between the executive director and company principals and among the executive director, benchmarking services team chair, and consultant have resulted in positive relationships and an ongoing commitment to providing quality benchmarking services to housing professionals.

Application of Benchmarking in Student Housing

Benchmarking has been implemented successfully at several institutions.

University of Minnesota–Twin Cities. The university has been participating in a resident study since 1998. Benchmarking data is shared with housing and residential life and university dining service staff to both measure satisfaction and progress and to plan for change.

The university dining service has used the data well. The university entered into a management agreement in January 1998 and noted a number of improvements in customer satisfaction shortly thereafter. In 2001, perceptions of improvement in quality increased by 23 percent after dining services enhanced menus, introduced cooking in front of students at a theme station, and improved salad bars, among other things. Additional plans include introducing pizza stations in three dining centers and standardizing the menu in all six residential dining locations.

Satisfaction with dining facility hours has increased 30 percent from 1998. The department has made considerable strides by increasing service hours in all locations for dinner and most locations for lunch. One dining center also implemented a continuous dining concept—from 7 A.M. to 7 P.M. Another location may implement continuous dining, and dining hours may be extended to midnight at yet another center.

Food plan options have increased 26 percent since 1998. In 1998, the department had very basic plans (twenty-one, nineteen, fourteen, and ten meals per week). In 2001, meal plans included a flex dine (food dollar) component, in which students pay a certain amount and use those credits to buy whatever meals they want. In addition, students can use the plan to buy items at campus retail operations. Also available are a block plan (students buy a certain number of meals per semester instead of per week so they don't feel like they are losing meals each week) and an unlimited plan, in which students can eat as many times as they want and as much as they want any day.

Changes in staffing patterns also addressed a number of issues, including computing facilities in the residence halls. Rather than let the residential life programmer run the resident hall computer labs, the housing and residential life department created a new position: coordinator of residence hall technology. The person in this position lobbied for more improvements in the computer labs. Student satisfaction improved by 16 percent from 1998 to 2001.

Another issue staffing patterns addressed was safety in student rooms. In 1998, students hired by housing and residential life (night managers) patrolled the halls during the evening hours. These positions have been eliminated: the University of Minnesota Police Department security monitor staff (also student employees, but trained and supervised by the police) patrol the residence halls. Student satisfaction has increased 10 percent since 1998. The police department is paid for this service. The use of security monitors as well as an increase in the number of community advisors also has had an impact on the increased student satisfaction in safety and security.

University of North Carolina–Chapel Hill. At the University of North Carolina–Chapel Hill, student satisfaction surveys are a vital part of providing service to residents. Over the years surveys and focus groups have been used to study the quality of life, theme housing, staff satisfaction, and so forth. The challenge faced by administrators has been in compiling questions, disseminating, and analyzing data, and, most important, responding to the data.

UNC Chapel Hill formed a partnership with ACUHO-I in using the EBI survey document and has completed its fourth cycle. The ease of using the survey instrument and compilation of results permit staff to do what they do best—oversee student education and facilities. Time is spent in translating desired outcomes into actions. Two major areas have been the focus of recent study: student education and support, and community and facility renewal. Both have received critical attention over the past several years, and results are readily apparent in the responses from students.

Rochester Institute of Technology. The institute has participated in various benchmarking surveys since 1998, including the resident survey, the RA survey, the apartment survey (twice), and the administrative survey (once). Results are shared with the vice president of student affairs, the residence life management team, as well as other staff members.

One of the main areas of concern was the retention of RAs; the results of the survey led to a revamping of RA training and compensation. These changes have improved the retention and caliber of RAs. The emphasis in RA training is focused on a grounding in student development theory and preparation for functional areas. Professional staff training has also been reviewed, with a strong emphasis being placed on current issues in student affairs and student development theory.

Future initiatives include using the data to engage in original research and writing articles, as well as presenting information from the benchmarking research to academic deans and academic program advisors.

University of Arkansas–Fayetteville. Staff have used a resident satisfaction survey as a tool to

- Evaluate job descriptions of RAs and professional staff
- Change the RA role to focus on interpersonal relationships, connecting residents to campus
- Monitor perception of safety
- Evaluate communication with residents
- Assist in designing new housing

Staff also have used articles in the *Talking Stick* on the RA study, even when they have not participated in it, to initiate discussions with their RAs about their position.

Summary

Benchmarking has proven to be an effective way to improve services and programs within student affairs and student housing. Benchmarking can assist with uncertainty and rapid change through the discovery of best practices, greater efficiencies, and a clearer understanding of what works most effectively. Benchmarking practices have been of significant benefit to student affairs and student housing programs that have applied the results of their studies and have improved the educational experience of students. Several professional associations including NACUBO, NACUFS, and ACUHO-I have provided leadership to their members by developing and implementing benchmarking projects. Whereas individual institutions have also carried out benchmarking surveys, the larger-scale benchmarking projects have been carried out through the coordination of professional associations and the assistance of consulting firms such EBI.

The ultimate benefactors of the improved programs and practices within student affairs and student housing are the students in higher educational institutions. They have gained a better education through the more effective delivery of programs and services as a result of participation in benchmarking surveys.

References

Alstete, J. W. *Benchmarking in Higher Education: Adapting Best Practices to Improve Quality.* ASHE-ERIC Higher Education Report, no. 5. San Francisco: Jossey-Bass, 1995.

Epper, R. M. "Applying Benchmarking to Higher Education." *Change,* 1999, *31*(6), 24–31.

ROBERT E. MOSIER is director of residential living, University of Wisconsin–Stevens Point.

GARY J. SCHWARZMUELLER is executive director, Association of College and University Housing Officers-International.

This chapter suggests how institutional leaders can use benchmarking to encourage employees, students, and faculty to effect changes in their colleges and universities.

Benchmarking as an Administrative Tool for Institutional Leaders

Barbara E. Bender

The first seven chapters of this volume discuss benchmarking in various services and functions of higher education organizations. This chapter focuses on the role of college and university leaders in developing and using benchmarking practices to promote institutional change.

Historically, colleges and universities have been viewed as trendsetters and change agents for society at large. They provided leadership in creating and developing products, in basic scientific research, and in advancing scholarship. In the modern era, or what might affectionately be called the technologically supported management era, leadership in advancing organizational development and modernizing management techniques has moved to the business community. Indeed, when it comes to the internal organization or management activities of colleges and universities, they more often resemble battleships at low tide stranded on a sandbar, unable to move or alter direction when any change is contemplated. From a minor adjustment to an academic calendar to a major overhaul of the curriculum, effecting and implementing change in a college or university can be extremely difficult and often results in institutional turmoil.

Evaluating the Need for Institutional Change

Institutional evolution through planned change processes is an organizational imperative. An institution that does not routinely evaluate all aspects of the organization and make the changes necessary to address its shortcomings, from the curriculum to the physical plant, is jeopardizing its future. Whereas performing organizational rituals in the same manner year after year may be comfortable for internal constituents and possibly even garner support from alumni (Kezar, 2001), those organizations that fail to evolve do not survive. Administrative practices, therefore, must be in place to accommodate the continuous evaluation of an organization's structure and procedures.

Learning what, if anything, needs to be changed is one of the most challenging aspects of making institutional improvements. Determining institutional direction through the use of deliberate and informed decisions takes time. Informed decision making, however, does not have to mean the extreme painstaking stalemates, or "paralysis by analysis," that can arise from conducting multiple and repeated studies, semester after semester. As with any research project, for assessment procedures to be effective, the correct issues need to be identified, the right questions need to be developed and asked, and the data need to be gathered and analyzed in a timely fashion (Upcraft and Schuh, 1996). Appropriate structures for enhancing collaborative decision making must be created, and a suitable course of action should be developed based on the data analysis that has been performed.

As Kezar suggests, "Change is not always good, and it is certainly not a panacea for all the issues facing higher education" (p. 8). Given the fact that the longevity of colleges and universities as organizations is due, in large part, to their adherence to their missions and traditions and the backing of loyal followers, institutions must carefully weigh their academic goals and strategic plans when they are contemplating changes (Kezar). It is essential to implement effective assessment processes to ensure that areas needing a mere adjustment, or even those operations that are dysfunctional, can be identified and addressed, while sound institutional processes and structures are supported and maintained.

Leading by Example

With the ever present demand for accountability and competing pressures from multiple constituencies for increased resources, effective and prudent academic leaders need to be thoughtful visionaries who can develop feasible solutions to institutional problems. The most important factor in effecting change, ultimately, is the courage of the leaders to identify an institution's shortcomings, then convey the findings, with potential solutions, to an audience that will include both proponents and adversaries.

Shaw notes that "leaders must direct the assessment effort to identify where the problems lie and what problems are perceived by the people who run the organization" (1999, p. 35). In many organizations, a change in institutional culture will be required to foster an ethos that promotes the provision of quality service across the institution. Operational changes, for example, though requiring a deviation from an institution's normal practices, can be effected with the motivation and dedication of leaders who are willing to adopt the new practices. Not only must leaders promulgate the expectations for excellence in institutional practice and ensure that high standards are the norm for the organization, they must do so by setting the example through their own behavior.

As suggested by Lampikoski and Emden, "Messages from management are not enough to maintain innovative behaviour. A leader must behave consistently in ways which will support credos" (1996, p. 134). The values and attitudes that are embraced by an institution's leaders, as reflected by the work and management of their own offices, will filter through the entire organization and help define the institutional standard. If the senior leaders embrace and promote benchmarking as an instrument to effect change, therefore, the practice will become a part of the organizational culture. When an institution is revising its expectations and procedures to adapt the successful practices of a peer or benchmark institution, the vision and enthusiasm of the leaders is critically important.

Overcoming Resistance to Change

Leaders need to create the organizational networks and relationships to prevail over those individuals and groups that join forces to defeat a proposed change (Kezar, 2001). Commenting on the perils of implementing change, Alstete observes that "benchmarking can help overcome resistance to change that can be very strong in conservative organizations, such as colleges and universities, that have had little operational change in many years" (1995, p. 25). When institutional leaders use benchmarking effectively, they not only can make changes more easily, they can turn the reluctant adversary into a proponent of the new initiative. Benchmarking can help smooth the path for those in leadership roles during the planning and implementation phases of a new organizational function or policy.

A goal may be readily obtainable, but it will require the constant encouragement of those who will implement the organization's new practices. As suggested in *Quality Assurance in Student Affairs: Role and Commitments of NASPA*, "quality in education programs and services in higher education begins and ends with individuals. . . . the people of the institution who deliver the educational programs and services" (National Association of Student Personnel Administrators, 2001, p. 3). Whereas extensive consultation is time consuming, collaborative planning and decision making will yield far more effective results than decisions that are made in a vacuum. Writing in *A Culture for Academic Excellence*, Freed, Klugman, and Fife note that "a quality culture needs leaders who involve and empower employees in continually improving processes" (1997, p. 37).

Successful transformational leaders, through motivating others, are frequently able to accomplish more than they had intended, achieving goals that would not have been obtainable with less effective leaders (Bass and Avolio, 1994). Setting lofty goals may not always be entirely realistic, but the right amount of cheerleading can be an effective catalyst to help transform an organization's operational culture.

Leadership Styles

In discussing social cognitive theory in organizations and the opportunity for vicarious learning, Sims and Lorenzi suggest that "The ability of individuals to learn by observing others enables them to avoid needless and often costly errors" (1992, p. 142). In fact, it is not unusual for newly appointed senior academic leaders to review and compare the practices of their counterparts at benchmark institutions to learn from their colleagues' successes and failures. Those who are new to their leadership roles, however, must be cautious when they are identifying which leaders they should consider as comparators, or benchmarks, in terms of leadership style. What works for one individual and institution may not necessarily be applicable for another organization. Student newspapers and the popular media can be useful, especially at institutions with a daily newspaper, to gauge reactions from a variety of constituencies to a senior leader's public decisions and programs.

Comparability of Peers

In Chapter Two Schuh correctly stressed the importance of identifying the right external peer group in benchmarking. Indeed, when senior leaders employ benchmarking techniques in making decisions, it is imperative that they use the right institutions for the right reasons. Using the appropriate institutions and programs as models, especially schools with higher reputational ratings, can generate an enthusiasm for change that can transform an institution. How many times have we heard the phrase that a college or university could become the "Harvard of the South" or the "Berkeley of the East" as administrators attempt to convince their faculty, students, and staff of the importance of implementing a particular practice? Using benchmark institutions as examples where different procedures or programs have succeeded can help reduce the tension and uncertainty that can arise when changes are being considered.

When benchmarking is used, the practices of peer universities must be studied thoroughly, and great care must be taken to avoid the mere adaptation of the practices of another organization. Every college and university has its own culture and organizational integrity; rote copying the practices of another organization can doom an initiative from the outset.

Benchmarking Locally for Quality Improvement

If institutional leaders willingly recognize the strengths of operations already existing within the university, their ability to identify internal peer groups for purposes of benchmarking will be enhanced. In many cases, when leaders are working with deans and departmental administrators, they will not need to go beyond their own institutions to identify organizations to use as benchmarks. Depending on the nature of the program or area being evaluated, comparisons with a peer group can be made within the same institution.

In academic affairs, for example, if the political science department needs to revamp its structure, it should provide the department chair with examples of other social science departments whose structures are working effectively. Similarly, in related administrative areas such as auxiliary services, or in student affairs operations, the internal offices with the best practices can serve as the benchmarks for other organizational units that need improvement. If it is the whole social sciences division that needs to be remodeled, using other academic divisions of the university as well as identifying divisions at peer institutions is most likely to provide the best sources for comparison. To guarantee the effectiveness of this process, institutional leaders must take the time to assist the organizational entity being reviewed to identify the appropriate benchmark to use.

In addition, identifying "best practice" departments with intra-institutional benchmarking recognizes those offices that are conducting their business in an excellent fashion. It acknowledges that the departments' efforts benefit the institution as a whole, and makes a statement of the institution's appreciation. Great care must be exercised, however, when identifying such benchmark departments. Leaders must be absolutely sure that the operation that has been identified as an exemplary department is really doing what it claims to be doing. The negative consequences of misidentifying appropriate benchmarks can be extremely demoralizing for other departments who recognize the failures of the weaker unit.

Campus Constituencies and Benchmarking

In Chapter Three, Loomis Hubbell, Massa, and Lapovsky discuss aspects of the admissions process and focus on establishing tuition rates using benchmarking. Comparability in admissions practices is critically important given the fact that prospective students, as a group, have been conducting informal benchmarking for years.

Applicants and their families, especially those who are informed consumers, compare everything that is sent to them during the college application process. They also study the information that is available through various World Wide Web sites, and exchange anecdotal data gleaned from current students and other applicants. Prospective students compare carefully the quality of service that the institution provides, remember which schools answered telephones cheerfully and returned e-mails in a prompt fashion, and, of course, weigh to what extent students are provided with financial assistance.

Educating Enrolled Students

Relying on the benchmarking skills they honed during the application process, enrolled students continue to use informal benchmarking when they compare their own institutions to those of their friends. From the menus and facilities of the dining halls to student life programming, academic and community facilities, curriculum, and even the academic calendar, student government leaders have always gathered reams of data about other institutions and provided those data to administrators in attempts to influence the practices of their own institutions. Astute administrators can use this practice to the advantage of the institution by training students in the art of effective benchmarking. Campus advisors should provide information to student leaders on which institutions the campus leaders consider to be institutional peers and the rationale for the assessment. Any such analysis should incorporate the institutional mission and the institution's ten-year goals so that students can understand where their proposed programs and alternative proposals might fit within the overall strategic plan. Students will be more likely to further refine their benchmarking research if they are taught the appropriate methods from the outset.

Educating Governing Board Members

Governing board members, perhaps more than any segment of the college community, including students, conduct the greatest amount of informal benchmarking. Using personal networks and reading about practices at other institutions in the popular press, they often champion institutional changes to mirror the efforts that are undertaken at colleges and universities that they perceive to be more prestigious or more forward-looking.

To resolve, or at least diminish, the institutional envy syndrome, the importance and role of benchmarking as a tool in institutional decision making should be included in new trustee orientation programs. These concepts should be reiterated in some form at annual board meetings but preferably more frequently. The trustee committee structure to incorporate decision-making models that use benchmarking approaches might be used. Special efforts should be made to acquaint board members with the institutions that are considered peers. Schools that are considered realistic competitors should also be identified with the reasons an institution received that status. In addition, trustees should be taught that various disciplines, centers, or programs might need to be benchmarked independently, given their unique or special mission within the organization. Board members should also have the opportunity to learn the importance of institutional comparability by studying institutional memberships in societies and professional organizations, funding practices, student and faculty profiles, governance, collective bargaining, mission, accreditation, and endowments.

Reducing Institutional Envy

Faculty, like students, have broad networks and many opportunities to compare their institutional programs and practices with those of their colleagues. Generally, discipline-based faculty, through attendance at professional meetings, participation in Internet listservs, and myriad other informal channels, can learn the most minute details about how other institutions operate. It is not unusual for faculty, therefore, to question why their own college or university has a problem with a particular issue or function when the matter could be easily resolved by emulating the practices of another school.

Once again, it is imperative that the leaders of the institution discuss the notion of comparability. Although in many instances gathering ideas and support in this manner can be very effective, the extent to which one institution's response to a particular issue is transferable must be weighed carefully, as in all aspects of benchmarking. Also important is the recognition that there will be disciplinary peer groups to consider, not just entire institutional entities. Not all psychology departments, for example, have the same academic or research foci, or even grant the same degrees.

Conclusion

Benchmarking can be enormously useful to influence and shape institutional decisions. Through analyzing the best practices of peer institutions, then adapting and developing programs for their own campuses, higher education leaders can improve the quality of programs and services that they provide.

Strengthening the effectiveness of a college or university may require altering institutional practices and transforming cultures and subcultures that have been in existence for decades. Even the most insightful and visionary leaders will require as many administrative support mechanisms as possible to succeed; benchmarking can be one such mechanism. Through the effective use of benchmarking, institutions can determine the degree to which they are successful as compared with their peer group, identify the areas they need to improve, and develop strategies that will work best for their unique organizational circumstances. Whereas practices and procedures are not necessarily transferable from one peer institution to another, learning from the achievements of peer institutions can be enormously valuable in strengthening existing programs and developing new initiatives.

All benchmarking efforts, of course, must incorporate and complement the vision and mission of the institution. It is up to the leaders to ensure that the college or university is working effectively to achieve its strategic goals, meet its accreditation standards, and realize its mission.

References

Alstete, J. W. *Benchmarking in Higher Education: Adapting Best Practices to Improve Quality.* ASHE-ERIC Higher Education Report, no. 5. San Francisco: Jossey-Bass, 1995.

Bass, B., and Avolio, B. (eds.). *Improving Organizational Effectiveness Through Transformational Leadership.* Thousand Oaks, Calif.: Sage, 1994.

Freed, J., Klugman, M. R., and Fife, J. *A Culture for Academic Excellence.* ASHE-ERIC Higher Education Report, no. 25. San Francisco: Jossey-Bass, 1997.

Kezar, A. *Understanding and Facilitating Organizational Change in the 21st Century, 2001.* ASHE-ERIC Higher Education Report, no. 4. San Francisco: Jossey-Bass, 2001.

Lampikoski, K., and Emden, J. *Igniting Innovation, Inspiring Organisations by Managing Creativity.* Chichester, England: Wiley, 1996.

National Association of Student Personnel Administrators. "Quality Assurance in Student Affairs: Role and Commitments of NASPA." Washington, D.C.: National Association of Student Personnel Administrators, 2001.

Shaw, K. *The Successful President.* Phoenix, Ariz.: American Council on Education and the Oryx Press, 1999.

Sims, H., Jr., and Lorenzi, P. *The New Leadership Paradigm: Social Learning and Cognition in Organizations.* Thousand Oaks, Calif.: Sage, 1992.

Upcraft, M. L., and Schuh, J. H. (eds.). *Assessment in Student Affairs: A Guide for Practitioners.* San Francisco: Jossey-Bass, 1996.

BARBARA E. BENDER *is associate dean of the Graduate School–New Brunswick and director of the Teaching Assistant Project at Rutgers University in New Brunswick, New Jersey.*

INDEX

121

Back Issue/Subscription Order Form

Copy or detach and send to:

Jossey-Bass, A Wiley Company, 989 Market Street, San Francisco CA 94103-1741

Call or fax toll-free: Phone 888-378-2537 6AM-5PM PST; Fax 888-481-2665

Back issues: Please send me the following issues at $27 each

(Important: please include series initials and issue number, such as HE114)

1. HE _____

_____

_____

$ _____Total for single issues

$ _____ SHIPPING CHARGES: SURFACE

	Domestic	Canadian
First Item	$5.00	$6.50
Each Add'l Item	$3.00	$3.00

For next-day and second-day delivery rates, call the number listed above.

Subscriptions: Please ❑ start ❑ renew my subscription to *New Directions for Higher Education* for the year 2____ at the following rate:

U.S.	❑ Individual $60	❑ Institutional $131
Canada	❑ Individual $60	❑ Institutional $171
All Others	❑ Individual $84	❑ Institutional $205

$ _____Total single issues and subscriptions (Add appropriate sales tax for your state for single issue orders. No sales tax for U.S. subscriptions. Canadian residents, add GST for subscriptions and single issues.)

Federal Tax ID 135593032   GST 89102 8052

❑ Payment enclosed (U.S. check or money order only)

❑ VISA, MC, AmEx, Discover Card # _____ Exp. date_____

Signature _____ Day phone _____

❑ Bill me (U.S. institutional orders only. Purchase order required)

Purchase order #_____

Name _____

Address _____

_____

Phone_____ E-mail _____

For more information about Jossey-Bass, visit our Web site at: www.josseybass.com

PROMOTION CODE = ND3

OTHER TITLES AVAILABLE IN THE
NEW DIRECTIONS FOR HIGHER EDUCATION SERIES
Martin Kramer, Editor-in-Chief